MODERN WORLD NATIONS

AFGHANISTAN
AUSTRIA
BAHRAIN
BERMUDA
CHINA
CUBA
EGYPT
ETHIOPIA
REPUBLIC OF GEORGIA
GERMANY
KUWAIT
IRAN
IRAQ
ISRAEL
MEXICO
NEW ZEALAND
PAKISTAN
RUSSIA
SAUDI ARABIA
SCOTLAND
SOUTH KOREA
UKRAINE

Saudi
Arabia

Robert A. Harper
Professor Emeritus
University of Maryland

Series Consulting Editor
Charles F. Gritzner
South Dakota State University

CHELSEA HOUSE
P U B L I S H E R S
A Haights Cross Communications Company

Frontispiece: Flag of Saudi Arabia

Cover: Adobe features at the Palace of Ibn Madi.

CHELSEA HOUSE PUBLISHERS

VP, NEW PRODUCT DEVELOPMENT Sally Cheney
DIRECTOR OF PRODUCTION Kim Shinners
CREATIVE MANAGER Takeshi Takahashi
MANUFACTURING MANAGER Diann Grasse

Staff for SAUDI ARABIA

EDITOR Lee Marcott
PRODUCTION EDITOR Jaimie Winkler
PICTURE RESEARCHER Sarah Bloom
COVER AND SERIES DESIGNER Takeshi Takahashi
LAYOUT 21st Century Publishing and Communications, Inc.

A Haights Cross Communications ◄━ Company

http://www.chelseahouse.com

First Printing

1 3 5 7 9 8 6 4 2

Library of Congress Cataloging-in-Publication Data

Harper, Robert Alexander.
    Saudi Arabia / Robert Harper.
        p. cm. — (Modern world nations)
Summary: Examines the history, geography, culture, religion, government, and people
of Saudi Arabia.
Includes bibliographical references and index.
    ISBN 0-7910-6935-4 — ISBN 0-7910-7176-6 (pbk.)
    1. Saudi Arabia—Juvenile literature. [1. Saudi Arabia.] I. Title. II. Series.
DS204.25 .H37 2002
953.8—dc21

                                                          2002007349

Table of Contents

Saudi Arabia

Camel herding was the livelihood of many Saudis for centuries, until the development of the oil industry flooded the nation with wealth.

Arab Tradition Meets the Modern World

S uppose you are a camel herder in the desert. You and your relatives live in a tent camp. You have no electricity, no plumbing, and you cook over an open fire. You have never seen a train or an automobile. You live mostly on camel's milk and dates. You cannot read or write. Because you are deeply religious, your children are taught how to live strictly according to God's law—a law that does not accept change easily.

Your life centers on finding water and food for your camels. In your search you move camp every few weeks. You have no radio, no television, and no telephone. Your only contact with the outside world comes when you visit town to sell your camels and buy some supplies or when you meet other tribes at a well.

WHAT TO DO WHEN YOUR TRIBE STRIKES IT RICH

Suddenly, outsiders who have different customs and clothes and speak a different language arrive at your camp. They offer you more money than you have ever seen to let them drill for oil in your part of the desert. The deal includes a payment for every barrel of oil they produce.

You agree. The strangers arrive with machines you have never heard of: trucks and drilling equipment, even an airplane. They do not want to live in your tent communities, and you don't want them, either. They build their own communities with their own type of houses and buildings, streets and cars, and their own food and lifestyle.

Not only do the outsiders find oil, but they discover that the largest supply of oil in the whole world lies under your land. At the same time, the demand for oil in the world explodes. Oil powers planes, ships, and cars; helps paves roads; is made into chemicals, plastics, and fertilizers; and powers electric plants. More people throughout the world begin to use oil products. Oil production from your land increases each year. More foreign workers, with their different ways, arrive. Some of their ways you like; some you do not.

Huge amounts of money roll in, not just to your country, but to you and your tribe. What are you, who never even had a bank account, going to do with this fortune?

You have money to buy anything your family wants; your nation can build cities, electric plants, water and sewage systems, roads, and airports. You can send all the children of your country to school for free; you can provide health care to everyone. What is not clear is how it should be done. How can it be done if you still wish to keep the religious and family values you treasure?

OIL MONEY: THE DILEMMA OF THE HOUSE OF SAUD

The above is not the plot of a Hollywood movie. It is a problem that has faced the family that rules the country of

Saudi Arabia since World War II (1939–1945). The money has brought not only great benefits, but also terrible problems and responsibilities. Massive changes have been made. There have been mistakes and there has been waste. The family was totally unprepared for the windfall of riches. Yet, it has made decisions that have changed the country. Today there are few wandering nomads. Most people live in large cities with modern facilities. Children go to free schools; there is free health care. Because of its oil and its role as the guardian of the holiest shrines of the Islamic religion, Saudi Arabia is an important part of two very different worlds: the traditional world of the Arab Islamic culture and the modern global world led by the industrialized nations of North America, Europe, and Japan.

The meeting of these two worlds in Saudi Arabia began less than 75 years ago, when oil was discovered in this Bedouin (nomadic Arab) kingdom. At the time, Saudi Arabia was one of the most remote and undeveloped parts of the world. Since then, the country has been a scene of tremendous change. It has also been a site of conflict between traditional tribal and religious values symbolized by the Bedouin Arab and the modern world imported to the country because of the importance of Saudi oil.

THE FAMILY THAT RULES

Saudi Arabia's struggle between traditional ways and the modern lifestyle came with the search for oil. The country's name, Saudi Arabia, comes from the name of the Saud family. Abdul Aziz Al Saud, or Ibn Saud, a desert chieftain, created the country by uniting many local tribes in 1932, before oil was discovered. The Saud family has ruled the country ever since. The country has no congress or parliament, no supreme court, no president, and no elections. Since 1992, Saudi Arabia has been a monarchy whose rulers can come only from among the descendants of Ibn Saud.

The king and his family control the whole country as well as the vast pool of oil and natural gas under it. They own the company that produces the oil; they receive payment for all the oil that is exported, and they decide how to spend that money—for themselves, for their country, or for religious causes.

CENTER OF THE MUSLIM WORLD

Saudi Arabia is the center of Islam, one of the world's great religions. Today, there are more than 1.2 billion Muslims, the name given to those who follow Islam, in the world. Muslims form the majority of the population in 39 countries that extend from Indonesia in southeastern Asia westward to Morocco, on the Atlantic coast of North Africa, and southward into Africa.

For all these people, Allah is the one God, and Muhammad is God's last great prophet. The words that God spoke to Muhammad are recorded in the Koran, the sacred book of Muslims throughout the world. Muhammad lived in the northwestern part of what is now Saudi Arabia from about 570 to 632. The Koran was written in Arabic, the language of Muhammad.

The Saudi Arabian cities of Mecca, the city where Muhammad was born and lived, and Medina, the city that first accepted Muhammad's teachings and that holds his gravesite, are the two most sacred Muslim cities in the world. Every Muslim is expected to make a pilgrimage to Mecca once in his or her lifetime. Millions of Muslims travel to Mecca—and on to Medina—each year. The Saudi government must organize the facilities used by those pilgrims and guide them through their holy rituals. The House of Saud, as the ruling family is called, sees its Islamic heritage as a sacred trust that makes Saudi Arabia especially important to Muslims throughout the world.

HOMELAND OF ARAB CULTURE

Arab culture, as identified with the Arabic language, had its roots in the Arabian Peninsula. That culture extends across North Africa from Morocco on the Atlantic coast to Egypt on the Red Sea. It reaches the heart of the Middle East in Jordan,

Lebanon, Syria, and Iraq. In this area, 270 million people are called Arabs, speak the Arabic language, and are Muslims.

A KINGDOM OF BEDOUIN TRIBES

At the core of Arab culture are the nomadic Bedouin tribes that, for thousands of years, herded camels, sheep, and goats on the desert fringes of the Arab world. These Bedouins were honored in Arab stories and myths, like the cowboys of America's heritage. Saudi Arabia is home to the most honored Bedouins, the camel herders. Like the Indian tribes of North America, the Bedouins lived in separate tribes in the deserts of the Middle East and North Africa. Arabia was made up of separate Bedouin tribes until Ibn Saud brought them all together to form Saudi Arabia.

SAUDIS: CONSERVATIVE AND FUNDAMENTAL

Saudi Arabia is one of the strictest Muslim countries. The Saudis are rich as a result of oil money. Still, they are tied to their very conservative Bedouin culture and religious values. As part of the Bedouin tradition, the Saudis are faithful members of the Wahhabi sect of Islam. It is one of the most fundamental and traditional of all sects. For the Saudis, there is no separation of church and state. The king and the House of Saud are believed to be carrying out God's law—Islamic law—as interpreted by Wahhabi religious leaders. As the Saud family modernizes their lives and their country, they must always consider what the new changes will mean to their Islamic faith. They feel that they must be very careful not to destroy traditional Muslim values.

THE GLOBAL IMPORTANCE OF OIL

In the 1930s, geologists from American oil companies (the Standard Oil Company of California and Texaco) discovered oil in the northeastern part of Saudi Arabia. Since then, scientists have estimated that oceans of oil lie under Saudi Arabia. Today, after more than half a century as the world's leading exporter of petroleum, about one-quarter of all the oil still known to be in the ground, as well as vast quantities of natural gas, remain under the surface of the country. Saudi Arabia has become a very important part of the modern world.

Oil accounts for about 40 percent of all the primary energy used in the world, and over half of that energy is used by the United States, Canada, Japan, and the countries of Europe. Japan has no oil production and most European countries have little, if any. Although the United States, the world's largest energy user, has oil, it still depends on foreign sources for almost two-thirds of its petroleum needs. Almost all of the oil that Saudi Arabia produces is exported to supply modern development throughout the world.

THE DIFFICULT TASK OF MODERNIZING

The modernization of Saudi Arabia has required a very difficult balancing of old values with new technology. Masses of non-Muslim technicians are needed to operate the oil fields, and to build roads, airports, hospitals, schools, and modern cities. Since the Persian Gulf War of 1991, there have even been American military bases established in Saudi Arabia. Wahhabi fundamentalists believe all these changes pose a threat to the Islamic faith. In 1996, a bomb killed 19 Americans at a military base in Saudi Arabia. Among the country's religious extremists is terrorist leader Osama bin Laden, son of a wealthy Saudi merchant. Most of the terrorists who attacked the World Trade Center in New York City and the Pentagon in Washington, D.C., on September 11, 2001, were of Saudi origin. Bin Laden and his followers have declared a holy war against the United States and have demanded that U.S. military forces be removed from Saudi Arabian soil. This holy war is also against the House of Saud and its efforts to change the country.

The conflict between old and new is one that takes place on the streets of Saudi cities and towns everyday. It shows up very clearly in the treatment of women. In Saudi Arabia—and much

Today, Saudi Arabia is a land of contrasts. A visitor might see women in traditional Muslim clothing shopping in modern stores or eating at Western-style fast-food restaurants.

of the rest of the Muslim world—women are heavily veiled and wear flowing robes when they leave their homes, so they will not attract the attentions of men from outside their families. Women cannot pray in the same room as men. They must be chaperoned when they shop or travel. They are not allowed to drive.

All this may sound like an attempt to punish women. To Saudi Muslims, however, it is simply part of their Wahhabi religious beliefs. For them, women are the heart of the family. As such, they must be protected.

Other rules prohibit all Saudis from eating pork or drinking alcohol. Wahhabis prefer that men dress in the flowing robes and the headscarves of Bedouins. They fear the corruption of outside influences. The country has no movie theaters, and the government controls television programs to protect the people from corrupting influences.

Saudis pray five times a day, facing the holy city of Mecca. In Saudi cities and towns, shops close their doors at prayer time. Whenever possible, people go to a mosque (Muslim religious building) for prayer.

With these restrictions, once can imagine the problems Wahhabis have with foreigners. Many people from other lands and cultures have come to work in the oil industry, or on one of the many projects the Saud family has begun to modernize the country. The Wahhabis want these foreigners—with their very different ways—to live in their own communities, away from the Saudi people. When the foreigners leave their compounds, the Wahhabis expect them to obey traditional Saudi rules. If they do not, religious police enforce those rules.

THE TEMPTATIONS AND DANGERS OF MONEY

Thanks to the billions of dollars that have been made through Saudi oil, the Saud ruling family—with 5,000 or more members—is now probably the richest in the world. They have spent money on homes in London, New York, and Hollywood, ski lodges, villas, and luxury apartments in some of the world's most costly and exclusive resorts. They travel in luxury cars and private jets.

They have also spent billions of dollars on a series of five-year plans to develop their country. They have tapped new water sources and developed irrigation works; roads, airports, and new industries have been built; even new cities have risen in the desert. The Saud family has also given loans to other Islamic countries.

Saudi oil is not only important to the countries and companies of the modern world. It is also tempting to Saudi

Oil rigs, like this one seen in an aerial view, have helped create the wealth of Saudi Arabia and especially its ruling family. Although oil has brought the country great prosperity, it has also brought problems as the nation has tried to modernize both its cities and its people's customs.

Arabia's larger neighbors, Iraq and Iran. Saudi money has gone into building a modern military equipped with jet aircraft, missiles, and tanks, so that Saudi Arabia can protect itself. To further protect itself, the Saudi government signed treaties with the United States. The Saudis gained support from the world's greatest military power, and the United States gained a constant flow of Saudi Arabian oil.

Over the past 50 years, Saudi Arabia has changed from a nation of poor tribal nomads to one of the richest countries in the world. During that time, the country has had to face countless difficult decisions. The major question has been: how to modernize while maintaining traditional Arab values. Trying to find the answers has put severe strain on the country's rulers and its people that continues today.

OLD AND NEW AS SEEN FROM THE AIR

Flying on a commercial jet airplane of Air Saud, the national airline, the contrast between old and new ways is clear. In the plane, on one of the in-seat stereo channels, the Koran is recited continuously. Passengers include Arabs dressed in fine, tailor-made suits and others wearing the traditional red-and-white Arab headdress and flowing robe. Some women wear the latest fashions, while others wear traditional robes and veils. In the rear of the plane is an area where Muslims can spread their prayer rugs. An electronic arrow points in the direction of Mecca.

As the plane approaches Jiddah, the busiest airport in the country, some of the basic facts about the country can be seen from the window. There is no question that this is a desert world. The land below is brown and gray, with barren upland ridges poking out. In the midst of this dry world, close to the city, are patches of green fields and rows of planted date palms, part of the newly created irrigated land. Jiddah itself is a sprawl of white and beige. The city center has a few modern high-rises, and much of the rest of the city contains closely packed apartment buildings three to ten stories high. From the modern airport extends a network of four-lane highways.

As the plane taxies to the modern terminal, high-rise hotels can be seen. The roads are crowded with cars and trucks. In one area of the field, the private jets of the Saud family can taxi up to the door of one of their mansions right at the airport.

In another corner of the airport, however, a gigantic tent covers several acres. There, people in traditional robes and veils are cooking over open fires, sleeping on mats on the floor, drinking coffee, and talking. Children run and play, dodging goats, donkeys, and camels. These are Bedouin Muslim pilgrims on their way to Mecca. They did not come on airplanes or ships; they walked or rode on camels, as their ancestors have done for centuries.

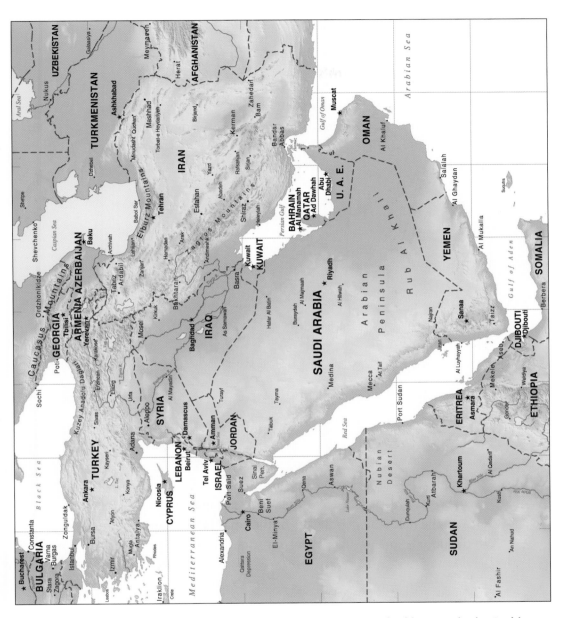

Arab culture, as identified with the Arabic language, had its roots in the Arabian Peninsula. That culture extends across North Africa from Morocco on the Atlantic coast to Egypt on the Red Sea. It reaches the heart of the Middle East in Jordan, Lebanon, Syria, and Iraq. Although it is part of Asia, Saudi Arabia occupies most of the large Arabian Peninsula that separates Africa from mainland Asia.

Saudi Arabia sits on the Arabian Peninsula, between the continents of Africa, to the west, and Asia, to the east. This view of Saudi Arabia was taken from space, from aboard *Gemini II*.

The Land:
Large But Small

Although it is part of Asia, Saudi Arabia really occupies most of the large Arabian Peninsula that separates Africa from mainland Asia. To the west and south, the narrow Red Sea and the Gulf of Aden divide the Arabian Peninsula from Africa. To the east, the Persian Gulf and Gulf of Oman lie between the peninsula and Asia proper. The southeastern portion of the peninsula faces the Arabian Sea of the Indian Ocean.

THE ARABIAN PENINSULA

Saudi Arabia makes up most of the Arabian Peninsula. The small countries of Kuwait, Bahrain, Qatar, and the United Arab Emirates lie along the Persian Gulf in the east. The country of Oman is located on the southeastern part of the peninsula, between the Gulf of Oman and the Arabian Sea. Yemen occupies most of the southern coast along the Arabian Sea.

On the world geopolitical map, Saudi Arabia is quite impressive. It is the largest country in the Middle East, and is much larger than any European country, except Russia.

The world population map tells another story. Most of Saudi Arabia has few, if any, people. In fact, a large area of the country is known as "The Empty Quarter." Although the capital city, Riyadh, is in the country's interior, most Saudis live close to the coasts of the Red Sea and the Persian Gulf. In all, there are only about 23 million people in Saudi Arabia, a population slightly larger than that of Texas, which is only one-third the size of Saudi Arabia. Each of Saudi Arabia's Middle Eastern neighbors—Iran, Egypt, and Turkey—has more than 66 million people, three times the Saudi population.

A DESERT SURROUNDED BY SEAS

Even though Saudi Arabia is surrounded by water on three sides, it is almost all desert. Less than one percent of Saudi Arabia is forested, and only one percent of its land is farmed.

The country is located near the center of the world's largest belt of dry climate. Arid conditions extend across North Africa's Sahara Desert, to the Arabian Peninsula, and into Afghanistan and Pakistan in south Asia. In central Asia, the parched landscape reaches the Gobi Desert that occupies much of the western half of China. Nearly all of this huge area receives less than 10 inches of rainfall a year, less than one-fourth the amount most of the eastern United States receives. The arid climate is caused by a huge high-pressure system in the atmosphere that lies over the area for most of the year. High pressure is associated with clear, dry weather, and rarely produces precipitation.

The Arabian Peninsula is separated from Africa and the Asian mainland by geological forces. The earth consists of

On the world geopolitical map, Saudi Arabia is the largest country in the Middle East, and is larger than any European country with the exception of Russia. But in terms of population it has only slightly more people than the state of Texas and is one-third the size of its Middle Eastern neighbors—Iran, Egypt, and Turkey.

a series of plates, separated by deep cracks that formed as the earth cooled over billions of years. Each continent sits on a separate plate. The Arabian Peninsula is separated from the main mass of the Eurasian Plate by a break that is filled by the Persian Gulf. There, the crack between the plates is slowly widening.

West of the peninsula, the Red Sea was formed by a crack in the earth's crust at the edge of a plate. This crack, called a rift, is the longest single break that can be traced over Earth's land surface—more than 3,000 miles. Its northern end forms the trench occupied by the Jordan River that flows between Israel and Jordan into the Dead Sea, whose shores are at the lowest elevation on the earth's land surface. The rift then extends southward to form the Gulf of Aqaba, an arm of the Red Sea, and the long, narrow trench occupied by the Red Sea itself. Finally, the rift continues southward across eastern Africa, where it crosses Ethiopia and Kenya, before it finally disappears into Mozambique.

Some of the oldest rock in the world is exposed in the western part of the Arabian Peninsula. It is very hard, having been changed by heat and pressure from deep within the earth over billions of years.

Uplands separate the Arabian Peninsula from Israel and Jordan in the northwest and from Iraq in the north. Mountains form an almost continuous ridge along the peninsula's western coast. Mountains are also present along the southeastern coast in Yemen, and border the southern part of the Red Sea and the Gulf of Aden. Here are found the highest mountains on the peninsula, rising just over 12,000 feet. The tallest peak in Saudi Arabia is 8,500-foot-high Jabal Ibrahim, located about 100 miles southeast of Mecca.

The peninsula is like a giant basin that drops away from high mountain ridges along the Red Sea coast to the low-lying shore of the Persian Gulf. In the middle of this great basin, in the center of the Arabian Peninsula, there are several long, low ridges that arc for hundreds of miles across the almost barren desert landscape.

PHYSICAL REGIONS

Geographers point out five physical sub-regions in Saudi Arabia. They are the rugged west, the rocky interior, the low-lying plains of the east, the northern border uplands, and the "Empty Quarter" of the south.

THE WEST

In the west, mountains stretch from Yemen and the Gulf of Aden northward to the Gulf of Aqaba and the border with Jordan. The continuous ridge forms the eastern wall of the Rift Valley that is filled by the water of the Red Sea. There are only a few scattered narrow coastal plains along the shore of the sea. Because it is formed by a huge geological fault, the shoreline of the Red Sea is quite straight, and has few good harbors. The Saudis divide the long ridge into two regions, based on important differences.

The Hejaz (The Northwest)

There are very few easy routes through the mountainous ridge between the coast and the interior. Because of the terrain and the difficulty of travel, the region is called the *Hejaz* (the barrier).

The western mountains are not very high. Some peaks reach above 8,000 feet, but most of the ridge averages about 5,000 feet in elevation. The region derives its name, "the barrier," not only because the mountain ridge is an almost continuous chain, but because it is tilted so that the western walls, along the Red Sea, are very steep. This has made it difficult for outsiders to enter the Arabian Peninsula from the west.

The eastern slopes are much gentler than those of the west. They form the upper part of the basin that extends across the Arabian Peninsula.

Short *wadis* (stream courses that are dry most of the year, but may carry torrents of water after a rain) have formed deep

The Hejaz Mountains (whose name actually means "barrier") can be found in the western region of Saudi Arabia, along the border with the nation of Jordan.

gorges, or gaps, in the steep western wall of the ridges, but few of the gorges pass entirely through the ridge. One gap extends inland eastward from coastal Jiddah to Mecca, then northeastward to Medina, in the interior of the basin. Jiddah, Mecca, and Medina are ancient cities located along trade routes that made use of the mountain gap.

Historically, the Hejaz has been one of the most important regions of the Arabian Peninsula. The trade routes between the eastern Mediterranean Sea and Yemen and the Arabian Sea to the south followed the eastern edge of the uplands. Over time, the people from this part of Arabia have had more contact with the rest of the world than have most other Arabians.

Azir (The Southwest)

South of the Jiddah–Mecca gap, small but important changes occur along the Red Sea. The mountains rise higher, but a narrow coastal plan has formed, making land travel easier. There, the climate is more subtropical. In the extreme southwest, near the border with Yemen, the ridge along the Red Sea joins the mountains of the southwest coast of the Arabian Sea. Here, a number of peaks reach more than 9,000 feet, with the highest towering just over 12,000 feet. One result of this region's higher elevation is that more rain falls here than in the Hejaz, or anywhere else on the peninsula. In fact, there is enough rainfall here to support the peninsula's only forests. Here, too, the valleys have long been farmed and the lower hills used for grazing livestock.

The most intensively settled area is along the narrow coastal strip called the Tihama. Along the Red Sea shore, the plain is salty from the tides. The rest of the lowland, however, has fertile alluvial soil washed from the mountains by rains and deposited on the flat plain. Good soil and adequate moisture are not the only advantages of this agricultural area. It is also the area of Saudi Arabia closest to the Equator. This combination of soil and heat allows farmers to produce tropical crops. The potential for growing specialty crops is so important that many of the mountain slopes have been terraced in order to create more land to farm. Many Arabs consider this area likely site of the Bible's Garden of Eden.

In Azir, the eastern mountain slopes are gentle. A number of wadis and rich alluvial soils have combined to create fertile oasis sites that are excellent for farming. Coffee has long been an important crop of the region.

NADJ (THE INTERIOR)

East of the Hejaz and Azir is a parched, mostly rocky upland formed of ancient crystalline rock. Parts of the region are covered with small sandy deserts and a few clumps of mountains, but rock covers much of the surface.

About halfway across the peninsula, two deeply eroded, relatively low, northwest–southeast ridges form an S-shaped barrier that crosses almost the entire country. Like the Hejaz wall, these ridges have steep west-facing slopes and much gentler slopes to the east. However, the ridges rise only a few hundred feet above the plateau, and there are gaps through-out them. The longest, highest ridge, called Jabal Tuwayq, is the source of water for a number of oasis towns.

West of the ridges lies the higher Upper Nadj. Here, there are no sedimentary rocks that might hold oil. A few long wadi valleys in the gentle slopes of the western mountains carry water that flows only briefly after an occasional rain. Some streams disappear into the dry ground, then reappear farther east. Even though the wadis are usually dry, when the water flows, much of it seeps into the ground. Wells are dug to reach this moisture, and provide water to oasis sites throughout the year. Most villages and towns in this very dry region are found near the wadis.

Protected by the mountainous Hadj in the west, the Nadj is surrounded by a different sort of barrier to the north, east, and south. There, a great arc of deserts makes travel very difficult. To the north, the Great Nafud (*nafud* means "desert") is covered with long sand dunes that are separated by valleys more than 15 miles wide. The sand gives the desert a reddish hue. There are several watering places, and scant winter rains bring short-lived grasses on which Bedouin herds graze.

East of the central oases that include Riyadh is the Ad Dahna, a narrow band of sand that extends for almost 800 miles. This area separates the heart of the Nadj from the coastal areas of the Persian Gulf. It is called "the river of sand." Winds keep the sand continually moving, and there are few watering places.

The Nadj is the heartland of Arabian Bedouin culture and the home of the House of Saud. Throughout history, it was occupied by many camel-herding Bedouin tribes and by some of Arabia's most important oasis towns and villages. The Saud family is from the area along the west side of the Jabal Tuwayq. Their most dangerous enemies lived in the large oasis of Ha'il, located in the Jabal Shammar Mountains between Riyadh and the northern desert.

AL HASA (THE NORTHEAST)

East of the interior slopes, the land is lower. It gently drops to the low-lying shores of the Persian Gulf. Here, the ancient crystalline rocks of the west are buried deep below sedimentary rock. It is these layers of sedimentary rock that hold vast deposits of oil. Much of the surface itself is covered with sand. Before the discovery of oil, this was a sparsely populated region, except along the coast of the Persian Gulf. The Saudis call the region *Al Hasa*. The name comes from a great oasis located here, the largest in the entire country.

Between the Ad Dahna and the Nadj is a barren, rocky upland about 70 miles wide. To the east, however, the coastal area along the Persian Gulf is mostly low-lying, rolling plain covered with a thin layer of sand and gravel. Bushes and sparse grass hold the sand in low dunes, called humocks, that give the land a bumpy character. The southern half of the Saudi coast is another belt of high, windblown dunes.

This lowland extends into Kuwait in the north and continues in the south through Bahrain and the United Arab Emirates. Boundaries between these countries are just imaginary lines drawn in the sand. Bedouins have long moved across them. Saudi Arabia and Kuwait have agreed on a "neutral zone" between them, where the countries share development and oil revenues. The continuation of the coastal lowland north into Kuwait and Iraq make the Saudi borders with these countries the most vulnerable to attack.

The Persian Gulf is shallow, and its water is dotted with offshore sandbars and coral reefs. As a result, there are no good natural harbors, although there are many small inlets that, throughout history, have provided shelter for *dhows* (small sailing boats). Only by building very long docks to reach deeper water can oil tankers be loaded at some Persian Gulf ports.

The sedimentary rock holds the vast pool of oil that has made Saudi Arabia so important to the global economy. The oil is great in quantity, is found close to the surface, is of high quality, and is close to the sea for easy export. Oil flows from many wells without pumping. As a result, petroleum can be produced much more cheaply than in most of the world's other oil fields. Oil has completely changed this region. In addition to the many oil wells, storage tanks, and pipelines, new deepwater ports and cities to house oil workers have been built. A large percentage of the residents of this region are foreign workers.

NORTHERN ARABIA

The Arabian basin also has a northern edge. Here, a high upland extends from the border with Jordan and western

Iraq. It rises to a height of 2,900 feet, and forms a drainage divide. To the east, waters flow into the Euphrates River system, once home to the great civilizations of Mesopotamia and Assyria, and today the heartland of Iraq. The uplands are covered with desert grass and scrub vegetation, and nomadic herders use them as pastures.

West of the divide is a depression 200 miles long, 20 to 30 miles wide, and 1,000 feet below the surrounding countryside. This basin is known as Wadi as Sirhan. Like the rift, it was created by shifting rocks.

The northern region gives way to the Great Nafud at its southern edge. The combination of rugged upland terrain and desert sands has discouraged settlement in the north. This empty desert does, however, form a good defensive zone against possible invasion from Saudi Arabia's northern Middle Eastern neighbors.

AR RUB AL KHALI (THE EMPTY QUARTER)

The vast sandy areas east of the interior slopes of the Nadj sweep southward into southern Saudi Arabia. The south is known as the Rub al Khali, "the Empty Quarter." This huge sea of sand, the world's largest, stretches for about 750 miles across the entire southern part of the country. It is nearly 400 miles wide where it merges with sandy areas farther north. The sand covers an area larger than France, Belgium, and the Netherlands combined. Some areas are covered with sand sheets, but there are also sand dunes that constantly shift with the howling desert winds. The winds fashion dunes into many interesting shapes, including mountainous ridges of sand 500 to 800 feet high.

The Empty Quarter is well named. It is so dry that there are few places where even camels or goats can graze. It was one of the last parts of the world to be explored by Westerners. It was not until the early 1930s that the first European explorers ventured into this hostile region.

Although there are great variations in the geography of Saudi Arabia, the land's most common feature is the extreme dryness and desert terrain for which it is best known.

EVER-PRESENT DRYNESS

The most obvious physical feature of Saudi Arabia is its dry climate. The country's aridity has produced the rugged terrain of the uplands and the vast sandy areas in the lowland. The landforms have been shaped by windblown sand and the erosive force of torrents of water following the few rains, as is common in desert areas. It does not rain often, but when it does, rain usually comes in the form of heavy downpours. There is almost no vegetation to slow the water as it runs off the desert slopes. Stream valleys that are normally dry become raging watercourses that tear away the land and move heavy boulders. These are the wadis. They pose the threat of destructive flash floods, but they also offer excellent sources of well water, which is important since Saudi Arabia has no permanently flowing rivers.

TRUE DESERT

Most of Saudi Arabia is true desert, receiving only three to four inches of precipitation a year. Significant rain occurs only in the mountains of the southwest, where as much as 20 inches may fall during a normal year.

No region has a real rainy season. A bit more rain falls along the east coast during the winter, the result of moisture being carried by winds from the Mediterranean Sea. An isolated storm can occur at any time, but thundershowers, particularly in mountainous areas, are more frequent in summer months. Rainfall consists of one or two heavy downpours a year. Wadis flood, then the water disappears rapidly into the earth. Many parts of the country may go several years without rain. In the Empty Quarter, in fact, an entire decade may pass without rain.

Windstorms often occur in June and July. Blowing over the vast areas of dry ground and sand, winds of 25 to 30 miles an hour, with gusts up to 65 miles an hour, can blow sand particles three feet or more into the air. Dust rises hundreds of feet. Like a snow blizzard in the U.S. Great Plains, sandstorms may make visibility impossible and may last for several days. It is winds of this kind that shape the rock outcroppings and keep sand dunes moving.

LESS DRY AREAS

Although the Tropic of Cancer, at 23½° north latitude, cuts directly across the center of Saudi Arabia, the only area that has anything approaching a tropical climate is the narrow coastal lowland of the Asiz, near Yemen. There, monsoon winds that blow water over the land produce most of the yearly rainfall between October and March.

The coastal lowland along the Persian Gulf north of the Tropic of Cancer has the feel of the tropics because of its high summer humidity, even though there is little rainfall. Such humidity often produces fog and dew—a substitute for rainfall. In most of the rest of the country, the humidity is almost always extremely low.

TEMPERATURE EXTREMES

Low humidity and mostly cloudless skies produce great extremes of temperature, from season to season and even from day to night, in the interior. Under the blazing summer sun, temperatures can reach 130°F. It is extremely hot from dawn to dusk, but at night temperatures may fall almost as low as 60°F. Because Arabia is on the fringe of the tropics, winters would not be expected to be long or cold, but at night temperatures in the northern half of the country can drop below freezing. Snow sometimes falls in northern Saudi Arabia, particularly in the mountains. It has even snowed in Riyadh, which lies deep in the interior of the country.

In such a dry country, much of the land is barren of vegetation. The vast areas of sand have virtually no plant life. In some places, a few deep-rooted shrubs with few leaves have adapted to the desert conditions. Many small flowering plants, dormant most of the time, spring into life and bloom during the few days after the infrequent rains.

THE IMPORTANCE OF WATER

In much of Saudi Arabia today, as in the past, the limiting factor for human life, as well as other animals and plants, has been the availability of water. Until oil production and modern technology came along, permanent settlements were located only at the few places with a reliable source of water on or near the surface. That pattern of settlement is gradually changing.

Bedouins, or "desert dwellers," are the traditional people of Saudi Arabia. For centuries, they have been a nomadic people who wandered the land with their herds of camels or sheep, avoiding most contact with outsiders.

CHAPTER

3

Bedouins: The Real and Legendary Arabs

Through history, most inhabitants of the Arabian Peninsula have been Bedouins (the word means "desert dweller"), who were skilled in utilizing the sparse desert water sources. To live, they have depended on animals—mostly camels and goats, but horses as well—that could survive under desert conditions. When they see the lightning of a desert storm, Bedouins move their herds and flocks toward it to take advantage of the small plants that grow for a few weeks after a storm. When there is no rain, they congregate around wells, where they draw water from deep below the earth's surface. In periods of drought, one Bedouin tribe might move onto land occupied by another tribe. There have often been fierce battles over grazing lands or wells.

WHO ARE THE BEDOUINS?

The term *Bedouin* is used differently by various people. Not all Bedouins were nomadic herders. City people refer to all villagers as Bedouins. There have always been close ties between the desert herders and villagers. Each has products the other wants. The camels, sheep, and horses of the Bedouins are highly prized in villages, and the nomads want the grain, dates, utensils, and other supplies they could get from villagers. In the past, nomadic Bedouins who engaged in camel trading or other trade might settle a branch of their family in an oasis. In fact, the Saud family, often considered Bedouins, was made up of villagers, rather than nomadic herders.

DESERT LIFE

Desert life produced a code of behavior. Since a traveler would die without water, the code says that any visitor—even an enemy—will be offered hospitality in a Bedouin camp for three days. After all, in the future, the Bedouins themselves might need the hospitality of others.

In a Bedouin community, the men look after the cattle and decide what moves the tribe will make. The tribe is led by a sheik, but his authority depends on the consent of the other tribesmen. Women are responsible for domestic life, finding fuel, hauling water, doing the cooking, raising the children, and even packing and unpacking tents during a move.

CAMELS: THE STAFF OF LIFE

Camels and goats are well-suited to desert life. Both need very little water and will feed on thorny plants, the leaves and twigs of desert shrubs, and dried grasses that other animals refuse.

The camels of Saudi Arabia are dromedaries—one-humped animals with short hair. They can live under desert conditions that are difficult even for goats. When the feeding is good, they store fat in their humps. This fat can sustain them when food

The dromedary camels of Saudi Arabia have long been vital to the lifestyle of the people, particularly the wandering Bedouins. Because the camels can endure extreme temperatures and can survive with little food and water, they were the perfect livestock for the desert Bedouins to raise.

is scarce. The fat not only supplies energy, but can be converted into water within the camel's cells. Camels have special internal mechanisms that are designed to make the best use of water. Their body temperature can rise as much as 6°F before they begin to sweat and lose body moisture. A camel can drink water that is high in salts and minerals, and convert it to milk. Camels can even recycle their urine. Thus, they can go without eating or drinking for several days. During such periods, camels may lose up to a quarter of their weight by dehydration without ill effects. They can regain that lost weight in 10 minutes by drinking as much as 25 to 50 gallons of water.

At the height of summer, when the supply of food for grazing is poor, a camel may need to drink every four days, but in winter when the pasture is good, a camel may go four to six weeks between drinks. During the winter, Bedouins do not worry about watering their camels.

Dromedaries are protected from desert sand. They have double rows of heavy eyelashes and hairy ear openings to protect them in sandstorms. They can even close their nostrils. They have a keen sense of sight and smell. With their short hair, they withstand extreme heat well. They even have large, soft, padded feet that work like snowshoes, allowing them to walk over drift sand without sinking. The camel's long neck allows it to nibble low-lying desert plants and also eat leaves from trees. The neck also gives the animal balance as it runs.

Before four-wheel-drive trucks and SUVs, camels were the freight-carrying "ships of the desert." Caravans of dozens of camels carried goods across Arabia between the Persian Gulf and the Mediterranean coast, to avoid the long sea voyage around Arabia and the length of the Red Sea. A single camel can easily carry more than 400 pounds. With their low water and food needs, camels were very cheap to use in the desert. A camel caravan could travel where horse- or ox-driven vehicles could not go.

Nomads who depended primarily on camels raised herds of 100 or more. The camels were not usually raised for food. Sheep and goats provided the Bedouin meat supply. Male camels were used as baggage carriers when the nomads moved, but most camels were sold in market towns along the caravan routes that skirted the edge of the desert. In return for their camels, the Bedouins received the dates, rice, bread, coffee and tea, and sheep and goats that made up their basic diet. Camel sales also allowed the nomads to buy clothing, tools, weapons, and even the goat hair used for their black tents. The replacement of camel caravans by trucks and roads forced many Bedouins to move to towns. There was no longer a market for their camels. Female camels were kept for breeding, and especially for their milk, which was an important part of the Bedouin diet.

FAMOUS HORSES

The Arabian Peninsula is also home to Arabian horses, famous for their intelligence, grace, and speed. Mounted on camels and these horses, the Bedouins raided oasis towns and settlements. Later, these raiders led the Islamic conquest of the Middle East and North Africa.

Today, the Arabian horse is highly prized throughout the world. The racing stables of the Saud family are among the world's most famous. Races are held in Riyadh each year.

SHEPHERDS

Camel Bedouins live in the drier parts of the desert. Closer to the desert fringe, where better pastures are found, the Bedouins are sheep herders. Their life is similar to that of camel herders. Sheep herders move their flocks from place to place, seeking pasture and water. Today, it is more profitable to raise sheep than camels. Both meat and wool can be sold in town markets. Sheep also reproduce more rapidly, and provide milk and wool for the Bedouins' own use. As vehicles replaced camels, some camel Bedouins shifted to sheep herding. However, like cattlemen in the American West, camel Bedouins have always considered sheep herders to be at a lower social level.

BEDOUINS FACE MODERN LIFE

As Saudi Arabia has moved into the modern world as a result of oil production and the development of cities, Bedouin life has changed. The Saudi government has tried hard to move the nomads into cities. Housing has been built for them, and they have been given taxis and trucks so they can do city work, as well as education to prepare them for city jobs. Many have adopted city life, but it has been hard. Some have tried to keep the best of both worlds, moving their tents, herds, and flocks to the edge of cities. Often, the males of the family will take city jobs, leaving the women to care for the animals and the family.

TRADITIONAL SAUDI DRESS

Men—*Aghai*, a double headcord worn over the *ghutra*, a flowing headdress (red-and-white-checkered in winter, white in summer); *mislah*, a flowing outer robe; *thobe*, full-length white, thin skirt-like garment worn under the robe.

Women—Scarves or woven head wraps that cover every strand of hair; veils; long petticoats under floor-length dresses with long sleeves and high necks; *abaya*, a long black cloak.

Some Bedouins still cling to the nomadic life. Even for these people, changes have occurred. Pick-up trucks now transport the Bedouins from place to place. The nomads have gas-fired cook stoves and modern weapons, but they continue to live in tents. The number of camels a family owns continues to be a measure of wealth. Bedouins who now live in cities still invest in the cattle, which are herded by members of their family who practice the nomadic life.

Over centuries, the Bedouins became skilled at knowing where a temporary water source and a bit of dry grazing land could be found at different times of the year. They learned the seasonal patterns of rainfall, changing their pattern of movement from year to year as the rains varied. They developed a system of movement, moving from wadi to wadi, well to well, sometimes spending as much as a month at a given water source before moving on to another. Their life was dependent on the desert animals that provided meat, milk, and hides for clothing and tents, even dried dung for fuel.

Even though only a small number of Saudis today still follow the nomadic lifestyle, Saudis are proud of their Bedouin heritage. The Saudi image of a real Arab is the Bedouin. The Bedouin is tough and resourceful; he practices true, traditional Wahhabi religion; and he is a savage fighter. Most of all, he is independent and free.

FARMERS IN A DRY LAND

Before the discovery of oil, there was little real agriculture in Arabia, except along the coastal plain of the Red Sea, in the nearby mountain valleys and the oases with large water sources. Where there was enough water, some crops could be planted. Date palms, in particular, could be grown in areas with very little water. Dates are a staple an Arab's diet, whether he or she is a Bedouin or city-dweller.

TAPPING NEW WATER SOURCES

With oil money and modern technology, new water sources have been developed. Once, wells could be dug only a few tens of feet deep. Modern well-drilling equipment can tap water sources that are hundreds, even thousands, of feet below the surface. Underground water occurs among the pore-spaces of rock, where liquid has accumulated over hundreds and thousands of years. In wadis, water may seep through the rock for many miles from the source of the rainfall. Such accumulated water sources are known as aquifers.

The most widespread aquifers are found in the areas of heavier rainfall in the mountains near the Red Sea. However, there are a few aquifers under the bone-dry interior of Saudi Arabia, where water may have been stored since prehistoric times. Other aquifers are supplied by waters that have fallen in the coastal mountains hundreds of miles away from where they eventually pool. It has taken hundreds of years for the water to move that far. Most of the aquifers of the interior are in pockets on either side of the S-shaped ridges that extend across the center of the country. The capital, Riyadh, is a city that was built over such an aquifer.

Modern deep-well pumps can deliver large quantities of water daily, enough for city use and also for irrigated agriculture in the middle of the desert. However, the aquifers are essentially being mined. Like the oil in the rocks, the water that has been in the ground all these years is being pumped out, and, like oil, the supply is not being replenished. The result is that the "water table"—the upper limit of the water in the aquifer—is being drawn down, so that wells have to be drilled deeper and deeper. At the present rate of use, these underground water reservoirs will soon be completely used up.

For Saudi Arabia, the water issue is critical to economic growth, and is an even larger problem for the future. Oil money has been used to find alternative water sources. The most likely source is seawater from the water bodies that wash the country's eastern and western shores. The ocean salt water is distilled in huge plants to produce fresh water. The process, called *desalination*, is very expensive and uses huge amounts of energy relative to the amount of water that is produced. The water made in this way is also flat and tasteless.

Most countries in the world do not consider desalination a practical idea, but the Saudis have plenty of energy and no alternative source of water. There are desalination plants along both the Persian Gulf and the Red Sea. Engineers have even considered towing huge icebergs from Antarctica as a source of water for Saudi Arabia.

Using the new deep groundwater aquifers, Saudi Arabia has undertaken a program to become self-sufficient in basic food needs, such as grain, meat, and milk. Wheat and other grain is grown with the help of irrigation. Cattle have replaced camels as milk sources. Saudis have learned to eat chicken that is

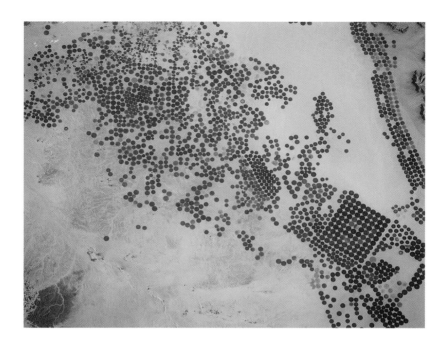

Because of the nation's dry conditions, little farming could be done without the aid of irrigation. These fields, photographed from the space shuttle *Columbia*, have been irrigated with the center-post method, using water drawn from up to 4,000 feet beneath the earth's surface.

mass-produced in air-conditioned poultry houses, as in the United States.

The idea was also to provide opportunities for the Bedouins who were being resettled. Free land and irrigation water were offered. There were interest-free loans for supplies and equipment. The government guaranteed prices far higher than world levels. Bedouins, however, did not like the daily work of farming. Today, most Saudi farms are operated by large agro-businesses that take advantage of government subsidies and the latest farming methods. Critics complain that large-scale farming has damaged the environment, particularly in drawing down the underground water supplies. Despite the development of new water sources, only about one percent of all of Arabia is currently farmed.

Saudi Arabia's city of Mecca is the center of the Muslim religion. Here, a large group of Muslim pilgrims to the city have gathered around the sacred Ka'ba, located inside the Holy Grand Mosque.

4

Saudis: People and Culture

The distribution of the almost 23 million people in Saudi Arabia is the result of many factors: the availability of water; the importance of Mecca and Medina as Muslim sites, and the importance of the port and airport of Jiddah; the center of govern-ment for the kingdom in Riyadh in the traditional Saud family homeland, east of the S-ridges in the interior of the country; the development of oil in the northeast, near the Persian Gulf; and the location of the one agricultural region in the coastal plain and nearby mountain valleys of the Azir.

WHERE THEY LIVE

Roughly one-third of the Saudi population lives near the Red Sea, most of them in the cities of Jiddah, Mecca, and Medina. Another third lives in an area centered on Riyadh, on either side of the S-ridge in the interior. The final third lives in the oil fields of the northeast, centered on the oil port of Ad Dammam.

Today, Bedouins account for only a tiny fraction of the population. Most Saudis—close to 9 out of 10—live in cities. Riyadh has more than 4 million people, Jiddah at least 2.25 million, Mecca more than 1 million, and Medina more than 800,000. In the oil-producing area in the northeast, Ad Dammam is home to about 1.6 million people.

WHO ARABS ARE

Saudi Arabia takes its name from its people and its rulers. The native people are Arabs, who are a very ancient people, even though the nation of Saudi Arabia itself is less than 100 years old.

Arabs account for about two-thirds of the population of Saudi Arabia. However, the Arabs of Saudi Arabia are just one part of the much larger Arab ethnic group that makes up most of the population of Iraq, Syria, Lebanon, Jordan, Kuwait, and Egypt in the Middle East. The Palestinians in Israel, Jordan, and Lebanon are also Arabs, as are most of the people of North Africa in Libya, Tunisia, Algeria, Morocco, and Sudan.

Ethnically, Arabs are Semites (the race to which Jews also belong), who apparently first appeared on the Arabian Peninsula long before the beginnings of recorded history. One of the Arabs' roots can be traced to the southwestern portion of the Arabian Peninsula, where Yemen is now; the other comes from north-central Arabia. Tradition has it that Abraham, patriarch of the Bible's Old Testament, was of the second branch. Abraham had two sons: Isaac, by his wife Sarah, became the patriarch of the Jewish people, and Ishmael, by his slave Hagar, became the patriarch of the Arabs.

TWO DIFFERENT TRADITIONS

The Arabs of the Middle East can be separated into two traditions: those who became nomadic herders in the desert, and those who lived in towns and villages, chiefly as either farmers, tending gardens of date palms, or traders who bought wool, sheep, and camels from the nomads and sold them.

The people in the towns learned about life in the non-Arab world through their trade contacts. The nomads, or Bedouins, on the other hand, had little outside contact, even with the nearby villagers. Contact with villagers was often limited to the times when the Bedouins raided a village.

The ways of the Bedouins of Saudi Arabia were very different from the civilizations based on agriculture that developed in Mesopotamia (now Iraq) and of Egypt. Both of those cultures used the seasonal floods of those rivers to irrigate crops, that producing great wealth and supporting large populations. Saudi Arabia has no such rivers. Tribes had to migrate from the desert to the wetter, fertile lands along the eastern Mediterranean Sea, as the nomadic tribes of the Old Testament had done.

As a result of these problems, the population of Arabia remained very small through the centuries. From time to time, one tribe or another would win control over neighboring tribes and form "a kingdom," but it in turn would soon be overthrown.

ISLAM: CENTER OF SAUDI LIFE

In the sixth century, Arabia moved from the fringe of world civilizations to the center of a major religion. The new religious movement began in the town of Mecca, an important trading center on the caravan route from the Gulf of Aden to Egypt and Damascus. There, in Mecca, the greatest and last prophet of Islam was born.

Mecca was already an important center of worship for pagan Arabs. As Muslims still do today, the Arabs worshipped a sacred black stone, the Ka'ba, said to have been given to Adam, the first man in the Bible, when he was forced from the Garden of Eden.

The people of Mecca worshipped many gods, but there were Jewish and Christian traders in the town as well. Muhammad, the prophet of Islam, rejected the pagan religion of his tribe and, as a merchant, studied the Christianity and Judaism of the merchants who came to Mecca.

In 620, when he was about 40 years old, Muhammad had the first of many visions—The angel Gabriel is believed to have come to him and told him "to recite for the Lord." Muhammad, who was illiterate, became a prophet for the god he called Allah, who was the god of Jews and Christians, as well. Muhammad saw Abraham, Moses, other Old Testament figures, and Jesus Christ as prophets. Muslims recognize Muhammad as the last and greatest prophet of God. He had a new message—the last word of God. Muhammad told the people of his tribe in Mecca to give up their pagan gods and accept the will of Allah. They not only refused, but forced Muhammad to leave the city. He fled to Medina, another trading town some 280 miles northeast, in 622. (The Muslim calendar begins with that year.) There, his message was well received.

THE MUSLIM CALENDAR

The Muslim calendar is very different from that of the West. For Muslims, dates begin with Muhammad's departure from Mecca (July 15, 622).

The Muslim year is lunar; it is based on the cycles of the moon. Since each cycle consists of 29½ days, the 12-month Muslim year is 354 days long (not 365). Every 30 years, the Muslim calendar has an extra day, like a leap year.

Because the Muslim year is 11 days shorter than a year based on Earth's rotation around the sun, the months gradually shift through the seasons. Over 33 years, a Muslim month will shift through the entire yearly seasonal cycle. For example, the month of Ramadan, when Muslims fast during daylight hours, will occur in all the seasons over 33 years. Since the observance of Ramadan requires complete fasting, including no liquid, during daylight hours, the duration of the fasting is greater in the summer than in the winter.

The days of the Muslim calendar are not determined by tables of the movement of the moon, but by the actual sighting of the moon, or daylight and sunset. Night begins when it becomes so dark that one cannot tell a white thread from a black one. Like any other month, Ramadan begins when the first new moon is sighted. In Riyadh during Ramadan, a cannon is fired to announce daybreak and sundown each day.

MUHAMMAD, MEDINA, AND EMPIRE

Muhammad preached that God was the ruler of the earth. Humans do not make laws; they must obey the laws of God as revealed to Muhammad.

The people of Medina soon accepted Muhammad's teachings and, as God's messenger, he ruled the town. Muhammad urged his followers to spread Allah's word to the world. Eight years later, he and his fervent Muslim believers had conquered Mecca. When Muhammad died in 632, he and his followers had spread his message across the deserts of Arabia. They had converted the desert tribes and established one government over most of the Arabian Peninsula. Within 12 years of the prophet's death, Muhammad's followers—most of them Arab nomads and townspeople—controlled most of the Middle East. Only what is now Turkey was not a part of the Muslim empire.

This rapid conquest was done by Arabs from the Arabian Peninsula who were driven by the power of their new religion and their enthusiasm for it. They were fighting a holy war to spread the word of God. They also were Bedouins, used to living under difficult conditions. They knew how to fight because they had regularly raided towns with populations larger than their own. They also knew the desert and, using camels and horses, moved forward along its edges to strike towns and villages. Their reputation as fierce fighters often encouraged communities to give up without a fight.

The Arabs conquered the Middle East, but they did not intend to destroy. They wanted two things: to spread Islam and to collect taxes from the occupied lands.

THE SPREAD OF EMPIRE

Over the next 500 years, Islamic forces spread across North Africa all the way to the Atlantic, then moved into southern Spain. They were defeated in southern France while trying to move into Western Europe. In the Middle East, they pushed

The prophet Muhammad, who said he had received the word of God, or Allah, made it his mission to spread his new faith as widely as possible. Although the people of his hometown, Mecca, at first rejected his ideas, the people of Medina supported him and helped begin the Muslim conquest of the Middle East.

back the Christian Byzantine Empire in Turkey and conquered the Persian Empire. The fierce Mogul tribesmen of central Asia (what was later the southern part of the Soviet Union), converted to Islam and spread their empire across Afghanistan into northwest India. Arabic traders sailed eastward across the Indian Ocean to bring Islam to the East Indies (now Indonesia, Malaysia, and the Philippines). By now, these forces, though still Muslim, were no longer led by Arabs, but by peoples they had converted to Islam.

The great Islamic empire of the past is gone. Even as it grew, power shifted from Arabia to Baghdad, Cairo, and other centers outside of Arabia. Still, the impact of what happened in Mecca and Medina dominates the Islamic world today.

THE TEACHINGS OF MUHAMMAD

Muhammad could not write, but his version of the words of God was collected in what became the holy book of Islam, the Koran (*Qu'ran*). For Muslims, the Koran is the holy word of God, as the Torah and the Bible are for Jews and Christians. The Koran, as interpreted by Islamic leaders, sets the rules of life for its believers, and for business and government in places that are Muslim. The Koran and the collected sayings of Muhammad (the Hadith) form the basis of Muslim law in countries where Islam is the official religion.

Muslim law applies to every part of daily life for individuals: what they eat and drink, how they behave at home and at work. The Koran tells a Muslim what he or she can or cannot do. Muslims follow it because it is considered God's law, not law created by humans. The main concern of government in Saudi Arabia is to enforce God's law. The House of Saud considers the Koran its constitution. Of course, it is humans who interpret God's word in the Koran, and therefore, God's law is subject to many different interpretations throughout the Muslim world.

Not only was Islam founded by an Arab, but the Koran was written in the Arabic language. As a result, Arabic has become the written language used in many of the countries that make up the Islamic world today even though Muslims in different areas may speak other languages.

The messages that Muhammad said he had received from Allah were recorded in the Muslim holy book, the Koran. This is a handwritten copy of that sacred text, which was made during the seventh century.

THE HOLY CITIES AND THE HAJJ

Wherever they are in the world, devout Muslims pray five times a day, facing in the direction of Mecca. All Muslims are supposed to make one pilgrimage to the great mosque in Mecca, which surrounds the ancient black rock—the Ka'ba—of Muhammad's time. Each year some 3 million to 4 million Muslims visit Mecca. The most sacred pilgrimage occurs between the seventh and tenth days of the holy month of Dhu'l Hijja, the time when Muhammad fled from Mecca to Medina. Each pilgrim wears the same white seamless gown, a symbol that all Muslims, rich or poor, are equal in the sight of Allah. The pilgrimage in Mecca lasts for a week. It is made up of both solemn worship and celebration and feasting. Handling so many pilgrims over such a short period of time is a tremendous challenge for Saudi Arabia. All the pilgrims must be transported, fed, and housed. Most enter the country through the port city of Jiddah on the Red Sea. They come by boat and plane, then must be transported some 50 miles to Mecca. Most pilgrims live in tent villages during their stay in Mecca. It is an enormous task to feed them all, provide sanitation and places to sleep, and even to communicate with people coming from foreign countries. Medical and first-aid facilities must also be provided, and the pilgrims must be guided through the many steps of the *hajj*, as the pilgrimage is called.

The House of Saud is very proud to be the homeland of Muhammad. Its members see their responsibility for assisting the pilgrims on the hajj as a God-given duty. At the same time, visiting pilgrims provide an important source of income for the people of the Jiddah-Mecca-Medina area.

King Ibn Saud, who united the tribes to create the nation of Saudi Arabia, began the ruling dynasty that remains in power today. Saud is seen here (seated) with his son, the Crown Prince Saud, who would become king upon his father's death in 1953.

CHAPTER

5

The Rise of the House of Saud

A rab leadership of the Islamic empire did not last long. There were too few desert people to keep control. The new leadership came from the ancient agricultural civilizations in Egypt, Mesopotamia, and Persia. There, Muslim converts became the rulers of great new Muslim civilizations.

RETURN TO THE BEDOUIN LIFE

The Arabs returned to their nomadic desert life but maintained their strong belief in Islam. There was no single government on the Arabian Peninsula; the people remained separated into different tribes, each with its own sheik and their own part of the desert, which they defended with great ferocity.

For hundreds of years, the tribes of the Arabian Peninsula were almost completely isolated from the rest of the world. They were few, very poor by world standards, and deeply suspicious of outsiders.

The history of the holy sites of Mecca and Medina was different, because they were so important to all the world's Muslims. They were first part of Egypt, and then, part of the Turkish Ottoman Empire. The holy cities were on the outer fringe of these empires, however, so the local Arab leader, the *Sharif* of Mecca, was largely in control. He became powerful among the very religious Arabian tribes.

THE ROOTS OF SAUDI ARABIA

About 1750, a religious leader in central Arabia, named Muhammad bin-Abd al-Wahhab, began to teach a very strict type of Islam. After traveling through the Middle East, he felt that Muslims had strayed from the true teachings of Muhammad. The form of Islam he preached was called Wahhabism, after its founder. Wahhabism spread through the tribes of Arabia, and Wahhab's followers began a struggle against the form of Islam practiced in the Turkish-controlled Ottoman Empire. Wabbahism further isolated Arabia from the centers of power in the Middle East. Early in the nineteenth century, the Wahhabis captured Mecca and ruled it for several years, until the Turks again took over all of northwestern Arabia, including both Mecca and Medina.

Wahhabism and its very strict interpretation of Islam remains the form most Saudis practice today. In Islamic Saudi Arabia, there is no separation of church and state. The king is seen as God's representative on Earth and the caretaker of the holy cities. The king consults a council of religious leaders on all major government decisions. Although Wahhabi values fit the way of life of Arabia's Bedouins, Wahhabism has presented difficulties for the present Saudi government as it works to bring the country into the modern world. For the Wahhabis, the world should ideally be kept as much like the world of Muhammad's time as possible.

THE HOUSE OF SAUD

The history of Saudi Arabia is not only that of Wahhabi Islam, but also that of the Saud family. The family comes from a town in the Nadj, 10 miles north of the present capital of Riyadh. Its members were supporters of the Wahhabi movement and gained power over other tribes with the help of its religious message.

Near the end of the nineteenth century, the Sauds were forced to flee the country and take refuge in Kuwait. According to legend, Ibn Saud (known in Arabia as Abdul Aziz), who would later establish the Saudi kingdom, was smuggled away in a basket slung from a camel as the family fled.

In 1901, as a grown man, Ibn Saud led a small band of men who captured the small town of Riyadh from another tribe. By 1912, he controlled the entire interior of Arabia. His goal was to capture Mecca and Medina. In 1924, he walked into Mecca. Wearing a seamless white robe, he entered the city not as a conqueror, but as a pilgrim. By 1932, he had taken control of most of the Arabian Peninsula and named his new kingdom Saudi Arabia, using his family name.

King Ibn Saud died in 1953. Since then, all of the rulers of Saudi Arabia have come from the House of Saud. The king does not rule alone; he consults with the other members of his family, who form the inner circle of Saudi society. All the kings of Saudi Arabia to this day have been sons of Ibn Saud. Princes hold the key positions in the Saudi government under the king. Ibn Saud alone produced a vast number of offspring—45 sons by 22 wives. This was part of his strategy to unite the tribes into one country. Each of his many wives came from a different tribe. Today, there are more than 5,000 members of the Saudi royal family.

The members of the Saud family, who essentially share political power over the nation, are always protected by a number of bodyguards. The closer someone's relationship with the family, the more powerful he or she might be in Saudi society.

THE FAMILY RULES

Because there is no parliament or other democratic body, the king is considered an absolute ruler. What he says is law. That is not really the case, however. The king's decisions must be acceptable to the House of Saud, particularly his many brothers, many of whom hold high positions in the government.

The authority of the king—and his brother princes—rests on a legacy of being children or grandchildren of the country's founder, Ibn Saud. Those who are farther removed from the main family tree have lesser government positions, or may control major businesses or military forces.

Foreigners doing business in Saudi Arabia know that it is important to have a connection to a member of the House of Saud. The wealthy Arab merchants and businessmen know this, too. Most of the rich made their fortunes through their connections to the House of Saud. Business is done in Saudi Arabia through personal connections, and there are no better connections to have than those with the Saud family.

Although Saudi Arabia has no representative government, the Saud family does not have absolute control. Its members depend on a wide consensus, both within the family and with the leading religious leaders (the *ulema*) of the Wahhabi sect, many of whom have married into the Saud family. The Council of Ministers that advises the king includes a few key princes and religious leaders, as well as a number of senior government bureaucrats. In 2000, the king established a family council of 18 senior princes to select future kings and to foster better relations between members of the royal family.

Because all important Saudi decisions are made by the House of Saud and the Wahhabi ulema, there is growing discontent among the educated Saudi commoners who work in the government and business. In recent years, the House of Saud has allowed these so-called technocrats to fill important government posts. However, princes of the House of Saud still control the key positions—defense, foreign affairs, and interior—in the king's cabinet.

STILL TRIBAL RULE

Ibn Saud began as a local sheik who ruled by consent of the members of his tribe. In an Arab tribe, every member can directly approach the sheik about any concern or to ask a favor. One of Ibn Saud's favorite quotations was, "The chief of a tribe is its servant." When he became king, he actually became the sheik over the sheiks of all the local tribes.

Ibn Saud lived a simple life and spent much of his time traveling from tribe to tribe with government records and the treasury in boxes, or receiving the sheiks in his palace in Riyadh. Any Saudi could visit the king to file a complaint; get a meal; obtain a dagger, cloak, or sack of sugar; dictate a marriage contract; have ailments treated; hear Wahhabi scholars recite from the Koran. Almost every day, the king held *majlis* (a reception) for any who wished to speak with him. Often he would feed several hundred such people.

To an extent, the Saudi government still works in this way. It has become a welfare state, based on favors from the House of Saud. Saudi people get free education through the college level, and even graduate school—in the country or abroad. Health care, including dental and eye care and prescriptions, is essentially free. Money is provided for those who need special treatment outside the country. Basic foods, such as grains, sugar, and milk, are subsidized, as are housing and utilities. Farmers and businesses receive grants and interest-free loans. Land on which to build homes has been given away. Land, cars, and trucks were given to Bedouins to encourage them to abandon their nomadic life and move into cities. A social security system provided for the elderly and the disabled.

BEDOUINS IN MODERN SOCIETY

The result of all this has left Saudis with little incentive to work. They rush to go into business, where they may become wealthy. However, few like to work for others or to work regular hours. They do not want to do the kind of physical work needed in the many construction projects—in the oil

By the 1970s, when this photograph was taken, the members of the Saudi royal family and government had already adopted many Western customs and fashions, as can be seen in the clothing of Saud al-Faisal, the Saudi Arabian foreign minister.

fields; on the roads, airports, and housing projects; and in city building—that are converting Saudi Arabia into a modern nation. They leave that type of work for foreign laborers, who are not, and never can be, Saudis, and cannot reap the benefits of the welfare state. Foreigners, even if they are Muslims, are expected to do their jobs, be paid, live in compounds away from regular Saudi life, and then leave the country when their jobs are done.

Oil is the only product that Saudi Arabia contributes significantly to the world economy. Therefore, it is important to keep the industry running efficiently. These workers are painting gas traps, which remove certain gases from crude oil. Painting the traps will help them reflect the hot desert sun.

CHAPTER

6

Oil in Saudi Arabia

It was the discovery of oil in the 1930s that thrust Saudi Arabia into the modern world just after the country was created. Actually, the first important oil discovery in the Middle East was by the crew of an Australian investor in Persia (now Iran) 25 years earlier—in 1908. This was the first well in the world's greatest oil-producing basin, which extends in and around the Persian Gulf. That basin is shared by the countries around the gulf: Iran, Iraq, Kuwait, Bahrain, the United Arab Emirates, Oman, and Saudi Arabia. The basin includes more than half of the world's known oil reserves still in the ground. Saudi Arabia has more than half of these vast Persian Gulf reserves.

In Persia, pipelines were built to bring the oil to the gulf, and a refinery was built along the coast. Oil from the Persian fields supplied fuel for the British navy during World War I. In 1927, oil was found in Iraq by European oil companies. In 1932, oil was discovered on the island of Bahrain, and geologists wanted to explore the lands of Kuwait and Saudi Arabia.

PERMISSION TO DRILL

Companies could not simply go exploring wherever they hoped to find oil. The countries of the Persian Gulf were sovereign states. The oil companies made deals that allowed them to drill in particular areas. As part of these so-called concessions granted by the government, the oil company paid royalties (a share of the price of each barrel produced) to the government.

King Abdul Aziz had offered a concession in Arabia in 1923, even before the nation had been created, but wells were never drilled. By the 1930s, American oil companies were very interested in exploring in the new country of Saudi Arabia. However, it was a time of great worldwide economic difficulty, called the Great Depression. Banks were having problems, and loans were hard to obtain. Oil was selling for 50 cents a barrel (it now often sells for more than $30 a barrel). An agreement was signed in 1933 that provided the Saudis with about a dollar for every ton of oil produced, plus yearly land rent of about $25,000. Provisions called for immediate exploration and the construction of a refinery once oil was discovered.

EXPLORING

The first area explored was what geologists called the Damman Dome, named for a nearby village. Today, the city of Ad Dammam is a city of 350,000 people and the oil capital of Saudi Arabia.

To aid geological mapping, a single-engine high-winged airplane was equipped with extra gas tanks and a big camera. Because of strict Wahhabi concerns about modern things, the government insisted that the plane fly high and use no radio. Blowing sand often grounded it, and it needed large tires to land on the sandy surface.

Before the first well could be drilled, bunkhouses had to be built and a pier erected to unload supplies. The first well did not produce enough oil to be used, but it did provide gas for cooking and enough power to drill other wells. After 15 months of drilling, the seventh well was a commercial success. The Saudi government received an advance of $50,000. In 1939, the first oil tanker was loaded at a new harbor on the Persian Gulf, with the Saudi king looking on.

Throughout the 1930s, geologic exploration increased the size of the known oil field. The geologists found the world's largest oil accumulation in a field over 160 miles long and 20 miles wide. To provide the funding and technical know-how needed to handle all this oil, the Arabian American Oil Company (ARAMCO) was formed. In addition to Standard Oil of California (SOCO) and Texaco, the original drilling companies, the Standard Oil companies of New York (Esso, now Exxon) and New Jersey (Socony-Vacuum, then Mobil) were added. World War II broke out in 1939 and when the United States entered it in 1941, all operations ceased.

THE MOST AND THE CHEAPEST

After World War II, production began to soar again. The demand for oil was growing rapidly, and Saudi Arabia was emerging as the most important exporter. Not only were geologists uncovering the world's largest oil deposits there, but the production costs were also very low.

In Saudi Arabia, the House of Saud owned almost all the land, and ARAMCO was the only company pumping. A few wells could be strategically located in each field. Large wells could be spaced miles apart. Each well fed into the same network of collecting pipelines, all of which led to one storage facility. Other important wells in Saudi Arabia flow freely to the surface without the need for pumping.

Even though Saudi Arabia was far away from the major world oil markets in North America, Europe, and Japan, shipment by ocean tankers was not expensive. A whole new deepwater seaport, Ras Tarnura, was constructed on the Persian Gulf, and a short pipeline brought oil to a second shipping port on the island country of Bahrain. The member companies of ARAMCO wanted to pump all the oil they could.

OIL FIELDS AND OIL

Oil is produced from 18 different fields in Saudi Arabia and five more in the neutral zone shared with Kuwait. The ARAMCO oil-drilling concession covers some 85,000 square miles, about 250 miles north, west, and south of the headquarters at the new city of Ad Dammam. It has reserves of more than 75 billion barrels, more than three times the total of all known oil fields in the United States. Oil is also pumped from the largest offshore oil field in the Persian Gulf. It has almost as much oil as the total reserves of the United States.

Saudi oil varies from one field to another. Some is light, some heavy; some "sour"(full of sulfur), and some "sweet" (sulfur-free). Light oils produce more gasoline and high-grade products; heavy oil produces more tar and asphalt. Oil in the ground is also associated with natural gas. For many years, gas could be piped to cities and factories in Saudi Arabia, but it was very difficult to ship by tanker. Most of the gas in Saudi fields was "flared"—burned into the air. Today, sophisticated gas tankers have been built, but the volatile gas makes shipment much more dangerous than oil shipment.

BUILDING THE OIL-PRODUCING SYSTEM

Although oil was plentiful and easy to reach, in the early decades of production, Saudi Arabia remained a very primitive country, and the desert environment was a very difficult place to work. An entire infrastructure had to be built, not just wells, pipelines, storage facilities, and shipping ports. Roads and housing for thousands of workers had to be constructed. All materials for starting the wells, oil-collecting pipelines, storage

To make oil production and shipment easier and faster, over the years Saudi Arabia has built several pipelines, like this one near the Persian Gulf on the north coast of Kharg Island, Iran. Such pipelines carry oil from the place it is pumped to the places it is refined and shipped.

tanks, and ports had to be bought in from North America and Europe. All the food and other needs of workers had to be imported. Warehouses, shops, recreation facilities, and offices also were built. And all construction had to be done in the hostile desert environment. All this added an expensive dimension to oil operations.

By 1970, there were about 10,000 workers; by 1980, the number was four times that. Thousands more people worked for contractors who were involved with the oil companies.

Oil production in eastern Saudi Arabia was on the wrong side of the peninsula to easily serve the North American and European markets. Moreover, Iran—no friend to either Saudi Arabia or the United States—lay along one side of the narrow Strait of Hormuz that separated the Persian Gulf and the Gulf of Oman. During the 1980s, Iran threatened to close the strait and attacked oil tankers in the Persian Gulf.

To overcome the problems of shipment from the Persian Gulf, two pipelines were built across the Arabian Peninsula. The Trans-Arabian Pipeline (TAP) in the north ran just outside the Iraqi border, across Jordan, to the ancient port of Sidon in Lebanon. When wars between Arab countries and Israel threatened the TAP, a second pipeline was built across the middle of Saudi Arabia to the new port of Yambu. These were the largest privately financed construction projects in the world at the time. Two additional pipelines—one for oil and one for gas—were later laid parallel to the one from the oil fields to Yambu.

Even with these pipelines, most Saudi oil is shipped from Persian Gulf ports. A second shipping port was created at Ju'aymah, 15 miles north of Ras Tarnura. Some 4,500 tankers are loaded each year.

CONTROL OF OIL PRODUCTION

The ruling House of Saud holds the rights to all the minerals in the country. In the early days of oil exploration, the country had no way of producing oil itself, so it offered the concession to explore to ARAMCO. In return, the House of Saud received royalties. As the global market for oil expanded after 1950, the royalty increased to 50 percent of the sale price of each gallon sold. Then, in 1988, the House of Saud took complete control of ARAMCO from the American companies. The Saud-controlled government now also owns the refineries and shipping facilities. ARAMCO also operates a fleet of more than 30 oil tankers, and owns storage facilities in the Netherlands, Singapore, and in the Caribbean Sea.

The growth of Saudi oil production has been phenomenal. From 500,000 barrels a day at the end of 1949, it rose to 4.8 million a day in 1971, to almost 10 million barrels a day in 1980. Since then, production has shifted markedly up and down, varying with demand.

As the world's leading oil exporter, Saudi Arabia has attempted to stabilize world oil prices or to use oil prices as a political tool. In 1960, it joined with other major oil countries to form the Organization of Petroleum Exporting Countries (OPEC), in which Saudi Arabia and its oil-producing neighbors around the Persian Gulf—Iran, Iraq, Kuwait, Qatar, and the United Arab Emirates—are joined by Arab oil producers in North Africa—Libya and Algeria—as well as Nigeria, Venezuela, and Indonesia. The group meets regularly to set quotas for each member country that will help world oil prices stay within a range that will suit OPEC nations. The production of Saudi Arabia, more than twice that of any other OPEC member, more or less determines OPEC's output. The problem for OPEC is that other major world exporters—Mexico, Norway, Russia, Canada, and Malaysia—are not members. This means that OPEC cannot completely control prices.

An official from ARAMCO, the company that has overseen much of Saudi Arabia's production since the discovery of oil, is seen here watching the work at an oil rig near Howta in 1997. ARAMCO is now owned by the House of Saud.

7

Creating an Economy Built on Oil

S ince its discovery more than 70 years ago, oil has produced more than $1 trillion for the Saudi treasury. This is an impressive figure for a country that, in 1950, was thought to have only about 6 million people. At that time, Jiddah, the port nearest to the holy cities of Mecca and Medina, was the only real city in the country. About half the people were nomadic Bedouins, living in tents and herding camels and goats. Most of the rest were oasis farmers trying to support themselves on date palms and small plots of grain.

SAUDI ARABIA BEFORE OIL

The chief exports were dates and Arabian horses. Arabia's chief contact with the outside world was with the hajj tourists to Mecca.

Taxes paid by the pilgrims were an important source of income for the House of Saud.

In this remote part of the world, slavery was not abolished until 1962. The first paved road—between Jiddah and Riyadh, the capital—was completed in 1967. Riyadh, an old walled city with about 30,000 people, remained intact until after World War II. The city consisted of two- and three-story adobe buildings with flat roofs. The tallest structure was a water tower. The streets were dry and dusty. There were open-air markets with tin-roofed and dirt-floored stalls; vendors cooked chickens over fires along the sidewalks. Nomads brought their flocks to the city with them. Public beheadings were held in the square.

The first Saudi king, Ibn Saud, kept the treasury in a trunk that he carried with him when he visited different Bedouin tribes. He handed out sums to individuals who brought their pleas to him. He regularly brought the local sheiks to Riyadh to receive religious instruction, and to keep their loyalty, he gave them subsidies. The government levied almost no taxes. Money came from taxes on pilgrims and from the British, who wanted to ensure that the Suez Canal–Red Sea route to India be kept open. When the first oil money began to flow into the treasury, the government did little with it. Other than building a few wells and a pier for the ships bringing pilgrims to Mecca, it spent nothing on roads, electricity, telephones, or any other part of a modern infrastructure.

WHAT TO DO WITH IT ALL

The oil money began to arrive in vast amounts after the mid-1950s. In 1970, annual oil sales equaled more than $500 for each person in the nation; by 1980, the amount was more than $11,000. Of course, the money all went into the treasury of the House of Saud.

Some of it was used to support a lavish lifestyle for all the

Despite the fact that less than a century ago even the largest cities of Saudi Arabia were little more than villages, today several Saudi cities boast high-rise buildings and other conveniences.

extended Saud family. Some was invested in banks, businesses, and real estate in the United States and Europe. Then, the House of Saud decided to move its country into the twentieth century. The first five-year plan, in 1970, was designed by Western economists who had been hired by the Saud family. More than $8 billion was to be spent, most of it on modernizing the largest Saudi cities, Jiddah and Medina, with streets, modern utilities, schools and hospitals, housing, and airports. Money was also to be spent on a modern defense organization complete with jet fighters and tanks. Other five-year plans followed, and expanded the settled areas of the country.

THE WORLD'S BIGGEST CONSTRUCTION SITE

Saudi Arabia became a gigantic construction site. Because the country had no factories to produce the construction materials, no engineers to make the plans, and no workers trained to handle modern equipment, the entire massive national development project had to be put into the hands of businesses and workers from outside the country. Contracts for the projects were given to large global construction companies from the United States, Europe, and Japan. The companies established project headquarters staffed by their engineers. Workers were recruited from other Arab countries—Egypt, Yemen, Sudan, Lebanon, and Pakistan—and from the Pacific Rim countries of Korea, the Philippines, and Thailand. They were hired by the tens of thousands. Airports had to be expanded to handle their arrival and housing for them had to be created on the construction sites. So much equipment was coming in through the few ports that ships had to wait off-shore for weeks, or even months, before they could be unloaded. In the midst of all this, the government also had to manage its new social programs. A wide array of departments—agriculture, defense, communications, finance, health, industry and electricity, interior, justice, petroleum and mineral resources, planning, public works, and housing—had to be organized by outsiders until the Saudis could get the education needed to handle the duties.

CONTROLLING FOREIGN WORKERS

The masses of foreigners, many of them non-Muslims, presented problems for the Saudi government. Islam has rules

Saudi Arabia continues to have mixed feelings about its foreign workers, who are so important to the economy. Although they recognize that Arabs can learn from workers like this American (left), they also fear that the influence of Western values and technologies may harm their traditional Muslim beliefs.

for everyday life—what to wear, what to eat, what to drink. Islam prohibited eating pork or drinking alcohol. The ways of the non-Muslims, particularly the Westerners who were in charge of the new construction projects and government agencies, were very different. The government decided to segregate the Westerners as much as possible. They were placed in housing compounds, with their own schools and recreation. When they left the compounds, they were expected to follow Islamic customs.

All this brought changes in the life of Saudi people, the majority of whom were Bedouins or conservative Muslims. Bedouins moved to the city, sometimes pitching their tents in any open space and grazing their flocks in the new public parks. In the cities, Western goods began to appear in shops; cars and trucks crowded the streets; fast-food stores, super-markets, and fashionable boutiques replaced the open markets and street vendors. Modern schools replaced religious schools where the curriculum had centered on the Koran. Saudi young people were sent to universities in Europe and the United States to learn engineering, economics and business, and international relations to help their country move into the modern world.

As part of the new development plans, all Saudis were given free education, health care, and social security. The government subsidized basic food needs, absorbing much of the cost of expensive food imports. Bedouins were offered free land, cheap irrigation water, and interest-free loans to buy machinery, seed, and fertilizer if they would settle on new farms. Others were given trucks or taxicabs.

The benefits of the new Saudi Arabia were restricted to its people only. None of the programs were available to foreign workers. Foreign workers are considered temporary residents. They are expected to leave the country when their contract is up. The Saudis expected that, over time, the construction would slow, and Saudis would take over the work. Then, Saudi Arabia would be made up almost exclu-sively of Arabs.

However, the foreigners have not gone home. Even now, foreigners make up one-third of the population and a larger

The contrast between old and new in Saudi Arabian society is quite visible in this photograph, in which Muslims are seen praying in their traditional manner beside a modern soft-drink dispenser.

share of the work force. There have been problems educating enough Saudis to take over all the management positions. It has been even harder to get Saudis to do everyday tasks: repairing the machines, and doing maintenance work and heavy labor.

Faced with the continuing importance of foreigners to the Saudi economy, in recent years the House of Saud has tried to bring change. First, it has increased the training of Saudis so that they can take over many of the jobs now being done by foreigners. Second, it has begun to make some concessions to foreign workers. Foreigners may now own land, and a compulsory health care plan has been started for them.

USING OIL MONEY TO BROADEN THE ECONOMY

As development plans moved forward, the House of Saud pushed to use its rich oil resources as a base for creating industry. The idea was to use the vast supply of cheap energy, particularly natural gas, which was being wasted as it flared in the oil fields. The first step was to build oil refineries, not only to supply the Saudi economy, but to ship higher-value products such as gasoline and jet fuel instead of the lower-value crude oil. Refineries also produce a wide variety of by-products that can be made into oil-based chemicals, called petrochemicals. Why not build refineries and petrochemical plants—and pipe the derivatives of the refinery directly to the petrochemical plants? Today, Saudi Arabia has eight refineries and several petrochemical plants. Most are located along the Gulf coast near the oil fields.

The problem is that, although Saudi Arabia has plenty of cheap fuel, all the equipment needed to build and operate its plants has to be imported. It costs much more to build a plant there than it does in the United States, Europe, or Japan, which are the major markets for petrochemicals, aluminum, and steel. Because of the costs of operation, the distance to world markets, and competition for these products, the Saudi investment in these plants has not been very successful.

EXPANDING AGRICULTURE

With the high cost of grain, meat, and dairy products, the House of Saud hoped to achieve self-sufficiency in the production of these foods. The Saudis particularly wanted to become self-sufficient in wheat, a staple of the Saudi diet. The government offered free land and loans for machinery, fertilizer, and seed, and a government guarantee to buy all the wheat produced at about 10 times the world price. Agriculture in the interior of the country depends entirely on irrigated water. Most is supplied by center-post sprinkler irrigation systems, in which a giant sprinkler sprays more than 1,000 gallons of a mixture of water and fertilizer each minute as it slowly moves in a circle around a center-post. The wheat program was quite successful, and in the 1980s, Saudi Arabia produced twice as much wheat as it needed. The government built grain elevators and storage silos to handle the surplus. With all the extra wheat, the government stopped the land-grant program and cut the guaranteed payment in half.

Other agricultural programs have emphasized growing vegetables such as tomatoes and cucumbers; improving the quality of sheep, cattle, and chickens; and expanding dairy production.

LOSING CONTROL OF WORLD OIL

Up until the 1980s, Saudi Arabia was able to control world oil prices. Since then, however, new oil discoveries in territories outside of OPEC member nations—in the North Sea, the Russian Arctic, and Africa—have led to great ups and downs in the international price of oil. Because oil accounts for more than 80 percent of the Saudi economy, the country has had both good times and bad. So much has been spent on both modernizing the country and supporting the rich lifestyle of the members of the House of Saud that even the great oil incomes are not enough when the world price falls. Despite all its oil money, Saudi Arabia today owes vast amounts to world banks.

NEW CITIES, BIG CITIES

The most spectacular change in the modernization of Saudi Arabia has been the rise of the urban population. Before the discovery of oil, the only large cities were Jiddah, Mecca, and Medina. Riyadh was a tribal oasis town. Today, Riyadh, the capital and home of the House of Saud, is an enormous metropolitan area.

The Saudis have invested huge sums of money to convert their traditional Arab towns into modern cities. Much of the new city designs depended on Western architects, planners, and engineers. Concrete and stucco buildings began to replace the adobe of the old Arab towns and villages. High-rise office buildings and apartment blocks similar to those in Western cities rose to the skies.

PEOPLE: DEVELOPING THE COUNTRY'S GREATEST RESOURCE

Perhaps the most difficult resource for the House of Saud to develop has been the people of Saudi Arabia. The issue has been how best to bring them into the modern age.

The government's first two five-year plans in the 1970s emphasized industrialization and the modernization of the economy. Since the 1980s, the emphasis has shifted to the people. Top priorities are education, health, and social services. Modern school subjects were added to earlier Wahhabi religious training. In earlier days, the children of princes and merchants were sent to universities in the United States and Great Britain. Now, new Saudi universities have opened. Education has been extended to girls as well. Today, almost 90 percent of Saudi men and almost 75 percent of women are literate. Universal health care has resulted in fewer infant deaths. Life expectancy is now comparable to that in some European countries. There are almost 300 hospitals in the country, and the hospitals in Jiddah, Riyadh, and Ad Dammam are among the most modern and best-staffed in the world.

All these programs were designed to show that Saudi Arabia was the equal of any nation in the world. With so much money available, architects and engineers could easily turn dreams into reality. Modern style was in fashion, but with a distinctive Muslim-Arabian touch.

Despite Western influences, Saudi Arabia continues to be the center of Muslim culture. These people, in their traditional white pilgrim's robes, are taking a rest during their journey to Mecca.

CHAPTER

8

Cities, Regions, and the Future

The large cities of Saudi Arabia are found in the three regions that contain most of the country's population: the Hejaz, along the northern two-thirds of the Red Sea Coast; the Nadj in the center; and Al Hasa in the east, back from the Persian Sea. Each region has a very different economy and is separated from the others by many miles of desert.

THE HEJAZ: THE LAND OF PILGRIMS

The Hejaz contains the holiest cities of Islam, Mecca and Medina, and the port-airport city of Jiddah, which serves as a gateway for millions of Muslim tourists each year. Saudi Arabia is proud that Mecca and Medina are the center of the vast Muslim world that stretches from Southeast Asia to the Atlantic Ocean and beyond to the Muslim communities in Europe and North America. The Saudis see it as their duty to protect Islam's holiest shrines and to provide Arab hospitality to the many pilgrims making their personal hajj pilgrimages each year.

The result is that the two holy cities are entirely Islamic centers. Non-Muslims are not allowed in either Mecca or Medina. Each is surrounded by a series of checkpoints marked by pillars about 15 miles from the city, beyond which only devout Muslims are admitted.

The means of making the pilgrimage to Mecca and Medina have changed greatly over the years, but the ritual remains essentially the same. In the past, most pilgrims came by caravan along three main routes. From the west, one route crossed from Egypt across the narrow isthmus between the Red Sea and the Mediterranean, then went south, close to the Red Sea coast of Arabia. A second route from Turkey and the eastern Mediterranean came out of Damascus and Jerusalem, and crossed the western edge of the desert on the Arabian Peninsula. A third route from Iran and Baghdad followed oases across the center of Arabia. Pilgrim groups were highly organized under a commander, who had the power of a ship captain. The caravan had guides and soldiers to protect the party from Arab raiders. There were cooks, animal handlers, notaries, secretaries, physicians, and even a judge. Musicians played marching songs.

With the coming of steamships and the building of the Suez Canal, pilgrims began to come by ship through the port of Jiddah. Today, some Bedouin pilgrims from all over Arabia and the Middle East still come along the caravan routes, herding their sheep, goats, and camels. Ships still bring pilgrims through Jiddah. Many of the pilgrims, however, come by air through the new modern airports at Jiddah and Riyadh. A whole terminal has been created for hajj pilgrims.

Mecca itself has no airport. In fact, no airplanes are allowed to fly over the holy city. All pilgrims must travel the 50 miles from Jiddah to Mecca overland.

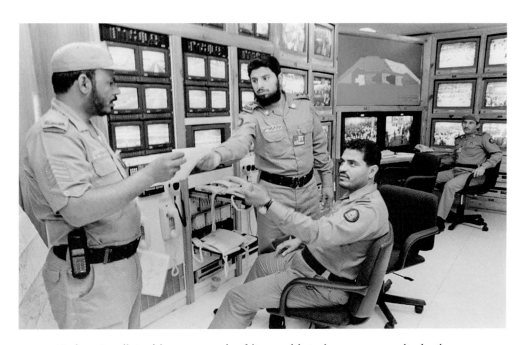

Today, Saudi Arabia uses much of its wealth to improve security both within and without the nation. These security officers are on duty to prevent violence during the pilgrimage to Mecca. The Saudis have also worked to strengthen their military, to protect themselves from outside forces.

Most of the 4 million annual pilgrims to Mecca come during the tenth month (Dhu'l) of the Muslim calendar, and usually between the eighth and seventeenth days of that month. Pilgrims can come at other times, but only for part of the rituals. Masses of people all gather to follow the same rituals. At times, there have been tragedies when people were killed after something caused the crowd to bolt.

In the center of the city is the sacred mosque of Mecca. Within it is a huge marble-floored courtyard to accommodate the crowds. In the center of the courtyard is the Ka'ba, a cube-shaped structure covered with a black cloth woven in Egypt that is taken down and replaced on the twenty-fifth day of Dhu'l each year. Pieces of the old cloth are sold to pilgrims as mementos of their hajj. The interior of the Ka'ba is empty except for pillars supporting the roof and a few gold and silver lamps hanging from the ceiling. In the eastern corner of the Ka'ba is the holy black stone that each pilgrim touches or kisses.

Mecca is more than a holy city. It is the administrative center of a district of the country. The Saudis have rebuilt much of the city, and there are apartment blocks and suburban homes as well as many hotels.

Many of the pilgrims to Mecca also proceed to Medina, 80 miles north of Mecca. It was there that Muhammad first started a Muslim community. In fact, *Medina* means "prophet's city." Today, the site of Muhammad's tomb in the Prophet's Mosque is second only to the Ka'ba among Muslim shrines. Muhammad himself helped build the mosque.

The city is in the midst of an oasis known for the production of dates and vegetables from irrigated fields. It has also been a center of pottery making. Although modern hotels and apartments and an Islamic University have been built, much of old Medina remains. Medina, too, is the administrative center of its surrounding area.

The city of Jiddah is far more than the entry point for hajj pilgrims. Since foreign embassies earlier were prohibited in Riyadh, Jiddah is the center of the diplomatic community of Saudi Arabia. It is also the closest port to Europe and North America, so many imports pass through the port, then move by road to Riyadh. Jiddah also has one of the largest desalination plants in the world, and an oil refinery that primarily serves its needs and those of Mecca.

The other important cities of the Hejaz are Ta'if in the highlands above Mecca, and Yambu, the oil-shipping port at the end of the pipeline from the oil fields in the east. Many of Mecca's workers live in Ta'if. Yambu is home to two oil refineries and a modern tanker facility.

THE NADJ

This is the traditional heartland of Arabia: the land of the Bedouin and the oasis farmer. It is also homeland of the House of Saud. Ibn Saud made Riyadh his capital and the most important city in the country. It remains the residence of the most senior princes of the House of Saud. It is also the country's center of government. Here are the headquarters of most of the government agencies that oversee the country's economic development and social programs.

Riyadh has also been made into the showplace of Saudi modernization. As the largest and richest of all Saudi cities, it has become a great marketplace of shops and stores. It has the finest university and hospitals in the country. With a majority of the motor vehicles in Saudi Arabia, Riyadh has a refinery to serve it other parts of the interior. Many of the country's largest private businesses and richest business families are based in Riyadh.

Riyadh is the focus of roads from other parts of the country and a railroad connects it with Ad Dammam, the oil center, on the Persian Gulf. Riyadh's airport is a measure of its connections with the rest of the country and the world. Although foreign embassies have been prohibited in the city, Riyadh is where the leaders of world governments and businesses come to meet with the House of Saud and the government. The city's modern airport is busy with the coming and going of government and business leaders. Many foreign workers also travel through it, as do some of the pilgrims to Mecca. Riyadh's population has sprawled out into the desert, beyond the city limits. There, suburbs have been built. Other oasis towns are also connected to Riyadh by modern roads. Buraydah and Unayzah, over 100 miles away from Riyadh, are cities with populations approaching 100,000. They are part of a series of oases settlements that extend along either side of the northwest–southeast ridges in the center of the country.

AL HASA

The region along the Persian Gulf has the third largest population concentration in Saudi Arabia. In the middle of the twentieth century, the area was sparsely populated. There were only a few tiny ports along the Persian Gulf and some oases settlements back from the coast. Bedouins roamed most of the land in search of grazing land for their animals.

Today, al Hasa is the most important part of Saudi Arabia's economy. It is there that most of the country's oil is produced. All of al-Hasa's major cities have been built as part of the oil industry. They are centers of well-drilling, pipelines, and refineries, and some are oil-shipping ports. These cities, which also house much of the population of foreign workers, are where the North Americans and Europeans and other foreign laborers take care of the various oil-field operations.

The largest city is Ad Dammam, one of the world's most modern ports. It has a population of more than 350,000 people. It was the site of an old port where small sailing ships traded with camel caravans along the trade route from India and Southeast Asia to the Middle East and the Mediterranean Sea. The remains of an old castle lies atop a coral reef close to shore. However, the harbor was insufficient for modern ships, so a new, modern port had to be built. That port stretches for more than seven miles along the coast.

Ad Dammam is more than an oil port. It is the chief Saudi port on the Persian Gulf. It not only receives most of the equipment and supplies needed for oil operations, but, with railroad connection to Riyadh, is also the receiving port for the country's capital.

Part of the urban complex of Ad Dammam is the city of Dhahran, the site of the country's first oil well in 1934. Dhahran was a desert in those days, but it soon became the site for the headquarters of all ARAMCO oil operations.

The first oil prospectors in Saudi Arabia landed at the

Ad Dammam, a busy oil port, combines the new technologies of the West with the traditional costumes and social practices of the Muslim faith. The women shopping in this modern marketplace are wearing *burkas*, with veils that may cover their faces and bodies.

small port of Jubail. At that time, Jubail was the base for a pearl-fishing fleet. It had the deepest harbor on the Persian Gulf, and handled cargoes for traders who managed camel caravans to Riyadh and other oases in the interior. Today, Jubail is the site of one of the largest industrial developments in Saudi

Arabia. In addition to an oil refinery, there are petrochemical plants, a steel mill, and an aluminum plant. The new port can handle large global freighters and tankers.

THREE SEPARATE REGIONS, VERY DIFFERENT IN CHARACTER

The location of the three population centers along the Red Sea coast in the west, around Riyadh in the center of the country, and in the oil fields of the northeast presents Saudi Arabia with great transportation and communications problems. Even today, Jiddah has no rail connection with the other two centers of population. Ad Dammam and Riyadh are linked by rail, but surface transport links are expensive to build and difficult to maintain in the severe desert environment. The easiest connections between the three population centers of the country are by air.

Each of the three population centers is also very different culturally. Life in Jiddah, Mecca, and Medina is focused on taking care of pilgrims to the holy city. There, the people are more concerned about the global extent of Islam than about Saudi Arabia itself.

At the other extreme, in the oil fields of the northeast, there is a very different international face to Saudi Arabia. If the west is the religious heart of worldwide Islam, the northeast is a secular world centered on producing and exporting oil and gas. This region is mostly populated by non-Saudis, and its output is geared to the technology and the markets of North America, Europe, and Japan. Production rises and falls with the price and demand for world oil. The largest share of its population are foreign workers, not Saudis. The Saudis want to ease into the international lifestyle that comes from North America, Europe, and Japan on their own terms, rather than be forced into it by foreigners living temporarily in their country.

The center of Saudi life is the Nadj, in the center of the country. This is where the Bedouin-Wahhabi tradition began and where it remains strong. Most of all, this is the home of the House of Saud and the capital city of Riyadh.

Governing the three very different population centers of Saudi Arabia is not easy. Even harder is balancing the strong traditions of Wahhabi Islam and the values of the modern global lifestyle. The House of Saud has managed to do this over the years, but not without problems. The religious Saudi conservatives do not like change. They consider many of the new ways an attack on their religion. Moreover, Bedouins are not interested in participating as workers in the modern economy. The routine of daily office or factory hours is completely different from the nomadic life to which they are accustomed.

THE FUTURE

The future of Saudi Arabia is unclear. As in the recent past, everything depends on oil. It is the one major product that the country contributes to the global economy. The Saudis have had only limited success trying to develop other industries based on oil. Despite the limitations of the Saudi economy, there is still enough oil for Saudi Arabia to maintain its position as the world's largest producer for about 100 years.

Some observers, however, wonder if Saudi Arabia and the House of Saud will be able to continue to control their oil. The nation's neighbor Iraq has already tried to take control of the country of Kuwait and its oil production. It is possible that trouble in the Middle East between the Muslims and Jews over Israel will draw Saudi Arabia into war.

Tensions in the Middle East are a major concern for Saudi Arabia. The formation of the Jewish state of Israel in Palestine in 1948 created problems for Saudi Arabia and the rest of the Muslim world. Palestinian Arabs, most of them Muslims, fled as Jewish settlers occupied the lands on which the Arabs had lived for centuries. Many of the refugees have lived in refugee camps in the surrounding Arab countries ever since. Most Arab countries have not recognized the legitimacy of the state of Israel.

The future of Saudi Arabia will largely be decided by the Saud family, whose members rule the nation. The Saud family has worked to make the transition to a modern economy more comfortable for their people. Prince Saud al-Faisal, the nation's foreign minister, is seen here after a meeting with U.S. president George W. Bush in November 2001.

As the richest Arab country and the site of the holy cities of Islam, Saudi Arabia has strongly opposed Israel. However, the United States, Israel's chief supplier of money and military equipment, is Saudi Arabia's main oil market. This makes for a tricky political situation at times, as Saudi Arabia develops its policies for the twenty-first century.

What about Saudi Arabia itself? Will the House of Saud be able to control the forces of both modernization and tradition? Will the young technocrats and other professionals continue to accept their second-tier position in their country? Will the Wahhabi fundamentalists rebel against the replacement of their values with modern ideas? Will the Saudis continue to depend on foreign workers—engineers, architects, and economists—to run their economy, and to do the jobs Saudis do not want to do?

Perhaps the biggest question of all is what the future holds for oil. In the past, the demand for oil and its price have gone sharply up and down each year. It is hard for a nation to make plans when it cannot know what its income will be from one year to the next.

The biggest uncertainty in regard to oil, however, is whether the world will continue to have such a huge demand for it. Already, alternative sources of energy, such as hydrogen, fuel cells, and even solar power, are being developed. If the world made a major shift to any of them, Saudi Arabia's global importance and wealth would diminish rapidly. It seems that the future of oil, the commodity that started it all, and that guarantees Saudi influence, is in doubt. Powerful tensions have also arisen between the new ways of industrialization and the honored Bedouin and Islamic traditions on which the country was founded. Saudi Arabia has become a world power, but its strength is threatened by dangerous instabilities.

Facts at a Glance

Official Name	Kingdom of Saudi Arabia; formed 1932
Size	1,175,349 miles—about one fourth the size of the continental United States
Urban Centers	(2001): Riyadh (capital, population 4.3 million); Jiddah (2.25 million); Mecca (1.2 million), Dammam (1.6 million)
Population	22.7 million (16.3 million Saudis, 6.4 million foreign nationals)
Growth Rate	3.0%
Religion	Islam (Wahhabi sect)
Language	Arabic (official)
Literacy	male 87.9%; women 74.2%
Infant Mortality	19/1,000 births
Life Expectancy	male 66 years; female 70 years
Work force	7.8 million (about 59% foreign workers); industry 10%, services (including government) 78%, agriculture 11%
Government	Monarchy with Council of Ministers and Consultative Council
King	Chief of state and head of government
Constitution	Koran; governed by Islamic law
Administrative Regions	13 provinces
Political Parties	none

Economy

Gross Domestic Product	$170.5 billion (2001)
Annual Growth Rate	1%
Per Capita GDP	$7,554

Trade

Exports $79.0 billion—oil and oil products (2000)

Imports $27.8 billion—manufactured goods, transportation equipment, clothing and textiles, processed food

Leading Trading Partners United States, Japan, Western Europe

History at a Glance

570	Birth of Muhammad
622	Muhammad flees Mecca (beginning of the Muslim calendar)
624	Muhammad captures Mecca
632	Muhammad dies
Late 1700s	The religious reforms of Muhammad bin abd al-Wahhab in Arabia; Saud family becomes the protector of Wahhabism in the Nadj
1880	Birth of Ibn Saud
1891	Saud family flees Riyadh and take refuge in Kuwait
1902	Ibn Saud recaptures Riyadh and begins consolidation of the Nadj and most of Arabia
1923	Ibn Saud agrees to first oil concession, but nothing comes of it
1924	Saudis capture the Hadiz and Mecca
1932	Ibn Saud establishes Saudi Arabia
1933	Oil concession granted to Standard Oil of California (SOCO)
1936	First productive oil well
1939–1945	World War II causes oil production to cease, but exploration continues
1944	ARAMCO formed between SOCO and Texaco
1948	Esso and Socony Vacuum become members of ARAMCO
1953	Death of Ibn Saud; his son Saud bin Abdul Aziz becomes king
1962	Organization of Petroleum Exporting Countries (OPEC) formed with Iran, Iraq, Kuwait, Saudi Arabia, and Venezuela as charter members
1966	Faisal bin Abdul Aziz becomes king
1970	First of five five-year development plans for the country begins
1971	Saudi embargo on oil shipments to the United States
1975	Faisal assassinated; brother Khalid bin Abdul Aziz becomes king

1980   Saudi government takes over ARAMCO

1982   Fahd bin Abdul Aziz becomes king

1991   Persian Gulf War against Iraq

Glossary

Ad Dahna: River of sand that separates Nadj from al Hasis

al Hasa: Eastern Saudi Arabia; the major oil-producing area and oil shipping ports along the Persian Gulf

Allah: God of Islam

aquifer: Underground source of water

Arabs: Culture group in the Middle East and North Africa whose members speak Arabic; Arabs include people of the Arabian Peninsula, Iraqis, Syrians, Jordanians, the majority in Lebanon, Palestinians, Egyptians

ARAMCO: The Arabian American Oil Company, established by Standard Oil of California, New Jersey, and New York, and Texaco to produce and ship oil produced in Saudi Arabia; taken over by Saudi government in 1982

Azir: Southwestern part of the country

Bedouins: Desert nomad tribes and related townspeople

Bin: Means "son of," also written "ibn"

Dammam Dome: First Saudi oilfield developed; site of the city of Ad Dammam

Ad Dammam: Largest city of Eastern Saudi Arabia; headquarters of oil operations

dromedary: One-humped, short-haired camel of Arabia

Empty Quarter: Vast, almost unpopulated desert of the south

Great Nafud: Desert area that separates northern Arabia from Nadj and the Hejaz

hajj: The pilgrimage to Mecca

Hejaz: Northwestern Saudi Arabia, where the holy cities of Mecca and Medina are located, along with the major port city, Jiddah

House of Saud: Members of the ruling Saud family, descendants of Ibn Saud

Ibn Saud (Abdul Aziz Al Saud): Founder of Saudi Arabia and its first king; father of all kings since

Islam: The religion proclaimed by the prophet Muhammad; the state religion of Saudi Arabia

Jiddah: Major port of Saudi Arabia; center of business in Hadiz; point of entry for pilgrims to Mecca

Ka'ba: The holy stone in the great mosque of Mecca thought to date back to Adam and Eve

Koran (*Qu'ran*): Holy book of Islam; considered the constitution of Saudi Arabia

Mecca: The holiest city of Islam; devout Muslims pray five 5 times a day facing Mecca

Medina: Second-holiest city of Islam, where the prophet Muhammad is buried

Mosque: Holy place of worship for Muslims

Muslim: Follower of the Islamic religion

Nadj: Central part of the country; traditional home of the House of Saud; includes Riyadh, the country's capital

oasis: Settlement around a water source in the desert

OPEC: Organization of Petroleum Exporting Countries, formed in 1962; current members: Iran, Iraq, Kuwait, Saudi Arabia, Venezuela, Qatar, Libya, Indonesia, the United Arab Emirates, Algeria, Nigeria, Ecuador, Gabon

Ramadan: Holy month in the Muslim calendar when Muslims fast from dawn to sundown

Riyadh: Traditional home of the House of Saud; capital and the largest city of Saudi Arabia

sheik: Chieftain of a Bedouin tribe

Glossary

Wahhabi: Follower of Muhammad bin Abd al-Wahhab, an eighteenth-century Islamic leader who preached the return to the values of Muhammad's day; Wahhabism is very traditional and anti-modern

wadi: Stream valley in the desert that is dry most of the time but often floods after rainfall

Yambu: Oil and natural gas shipping port on the Red Sea

Barfield, Thomas. *The Nomadic Alternative*. Englewood Cliffs, N.J.: Prentice Hall, 1993.

Central Intelligence Agency. *Issues in the Middle East Atlas*. 1973.

Foud al-Farsey. *Modernity and Tradition: The Saudi Equation*. New York: Kegan Paul International, 1990.

International Energy Agency, *Middle East Oil and Gas*. 1995.

Ismail Nawwab, Peter Speers, and Paul Hoye. *ARAMCO and its World: Arabia and the Middle East*. Dhaahran: ARAMCO, 1981.

Kaplan, Robert, *The Arabists*. New York: The Free Press, 1995.

Lacey, Robert. *The Kingdom: Arabia and the House of Sa'ud*. New York: Harcourt Brace Jovanovich, 1981.

Life World Library. *The Arab World*. New York: Time, 1962.

Mackay, Sandra, *The Saudis*. Boston: Houghton Mifflin Co., 1987.

The Times Atlas of World History. Rev. ed. Maplewood, N.J.: Hammond, 1984.

World *Satellite Atlas of the World*. Toronto: Warwick Publishing, 1997.

World Almanac and Book of Facts 2002. New York: World Almanac Books, 2001.

Websites

Economist Magazine: Saudi Arabia
www.economist.com/countries/saudiarabia/

Library of Congress: Saudi Arabia
www.lcweb2.loc.gov/frd/cs/satoc.html

U.S. State Department: Saudi Arabia
www.state.gov/r/pa/ei/bgr/3584.htm

Index

Ad Dahna, 29
Ad Dammam, 48, 66, 68, 83, 90, 92
Agriculture, 16, 18, 22, 27-28, 43, 44-45, 47, 48-49, 62, 73, 78, 80-81, 88, 89
Airlines, 18, 92
Airports, 16, 76, 85, 89
Al Dammam, 89
Al Hasa (Northeast), 25, 29-30, 85, 90
Allah, 12, 50, 54
Aquifers, 43-44
Arab culture, 12-13
Arabian American Oil Company (ARAMCO), 67, 68, 70, 90
Arabian horses, 37, 38, 41, 73
Arabian Peninsula, 21-24, 25, 27, 48, 51, 57
Arabian Sea, 21, 22, 27
Arabic culture, 53
Arabic language, 12, 13, 53
Arabs, 48
  and spread of Islam, 51-53
  and tribes, 57-58
Ar Rub al Khali (Empty Quarter), 22, 25, 31, 33
Asiz, 34
Azir (Southwest), 25, 27, 47

Bahrain, 66
Bedouins, 9-10, 11, 13, 29, 30, 31, 37-43, 48, 73, 89, 90, 92-93
  and camels, 9, 13, 37, 38-40, 41, 42, 51, 73
  and dress of men, 16, 18
  and food, 38, 40, 41, 43
  and gender roles, 38, 42
  and goats, 37, 38, 40, 73
  and horses, 37, 38, 41, 51
  in labor force, 42, 45, 62-63, 93
  and modernization, 41-43, 62-63
  and pilgrimages, 86
  resettlement of, 41-42, 45, 62, 78
  and sheep, 38, 40, 41
  and sheik, 38
  and spread of Islam, 51
  and tradition, 18

and villagers, 38, 40-41, 48-49
  and Wahhabism, 43, 58
  and water, 37, 38, 42-43, 49
Bin Laden, Osama, 14
Boundaries, 20, 21-22, 30-31
Britain, annual payments from, 74
Buraydah, 89

Capital city. *See* Riyadh
Caravans, camels and, 40, 41, 90
Cities, 11, 16, 18, 22, 27, 34, 41-42, 44, 47-48, 62, 68, 74, 76, 78, 82, 83, 85
Climate, 22, 27-28, 29, 32-34
Coffee, 28
Communication, 92
Council of Ministers, 61

Damman Dome, 66
Desalinization plants, 44, 88
Deserts, 18, 22, 24, 28, 29, 31, 33
Dhahran, 90
Dress
  and men, 16, 18, 38, 42
  and pilgrimage, 54
  and women, 16, 18, 42

Economy, 73-83, 90, 91-92, 93
  See also Oil
Education, 11, 62, 76, 78, 82, 89

Floods, 33
Food
  and Bedouins, 38, 40, 41, 43
  and chicken, 44-45, 74, 81
  and dates, 18, 40, 43, 49, 73, 88
  and Islam, 16, 53, 77
  and self-sufficiency, 44-45, 80-81
  and subsidies, 62, 78
  and vegetables, 81, 88
  and wheat, 44, 73, 81
Foreign aid
  from Saudi Arabia, 16
  to Saudi Arabia, 81
Foreign embassies, 88, 89
Foreign investment, 75

Index

Picture Credits

page:

15: AP/Wide World Photos
17: © Bettmann/Corbis
19: 21st Century Publishing
20: Courtesy NASA
23: 21st Century Publishing
25: © Charles and Josette Lenars/Corbis
31: Corbis
36: © Bettmann/Corbis
39: © Ric Ergenbright/Corbis
44: © 1996 Corbis
46: AP/Wide World Photos
52: Archive Photos
54: AP/Wide World Photos

56: AP/Wide World Photos
60: © Bettmann Corbis
63: AP/Wide World Photos
64: AP/Wide World Photos
69: © Roger Wood/Corbis
72: AP/Wide World Photos
75: AP/Wide World Photos
79: Hulton Archive by Getty Images
84: AP/Wide World Photos
87: AP/Wide World Photos
91: AP/Wide World Photos
94: AP/Wide World Photos

Frontis: Flag courtesy of *theodora.com/flags*. Used with permission.

Cover: © Jeremy Horner/Corbis

ROBERT A. HARPER is Professor Emeritus of Geography, University of Maryland, College Park. He also taught at Southern Illinois University, Carbondale and was a visiting professor at the University of Manchester, England; University of Sydney, Australia; University of Durban, South Africa; and Peking and Northwest Universities, China. He is past president of the National Council for Geographic Education and holds their George J. Miller service award and a Professional Achievement award from his alma mater, the University of Chicago. He is the author, co-author, co-editor of geography texts that range from second grade to university. In retirement he has written *The University that Shouldn't Happen, BUT DID! Southern Illinois University during the Morris years 1948–1972.* He has been married for 58 years and lives in Carbondale.

CHARLES F. "FRITZ" GRITZNER is Distinguished Professor of Geography at South Dakota State University. He is now in his fifth decade of college teaching and research. Much of his career work has focused on geographic education. Fritz has served as both president and executive director of the National Council for Geographic Education and has received the Council's George J. Miller Award for Distinguished Service.